IN OUR RIGHTEOUS MIGHT

Written By:

CHARLES VAUGHN

Copyright © 2023 Charles Vaughn.

All rights reserved. No part of this book may be reproduced, stored, or transmitted by any means—whether auditory, graphic, mechanical, or electronic—without written permission of both publisher and author, except in the case of brief excerpts used in critical articles and reviews. Unauthorized reproduction of any part of this work is illegal and is punishable by law.

ISBN: 979-8-88640-899-7 (sc)
ISBN: 979-8-88640-900-0 (hc)
ISBN: 979-8-88640-901-7 (e)

Because of the dynamic nature of the Internet, any web addresses or links contained in this book may have changed since publication and may no longer be valid. The views expressed in this work are solely those of the author and do not necessarily reflect the views of the publisher, and the publisher hereby disclaims any responsibility for them.

One Galleria Blvd., Suite 1900, Metairie, LA 70001
1-888-421-2397

CONTENTS

Special Thanks..v
Preface vii

Chapter 1   Just Getting Started 1
Chapter 2   A Day that Lives in Infamy...........................20
Chapter 3   A Time for Decisions 36
Chapter 4   Called to Duty...49
Chapter 5   In the Army Now 56
Chapter 6   Settling In 71
Chapter 7   Becoming One...89
Chapter 8   Change in Plans..106
Chapter 9   A Brief Homecoming.................................. 117
Chapter 10 A Home in the 678th Field Artillery 130
Chapter 11 Time to Cross the Big Pond 142
Chapter 12 D-Day and Beyond.....................................154
Chapter 13 Waiting on the News 167
Chapter 14 The Push Through Belgium 175
Chapter 15 An Act of Desperation 187
Chapter 16 Crossing into Germany............................... 196
Chapter 17 It Is Over 207
Chapter 18 Going Home... 217

SPECIAL THANKS

I dedicate this book to all who have made the sacrifice to our freedom through their service to this country.

Especially the selfless sacrifices that were made by our spouses who faced the hardship of us being deployed. They maintained the homefront allowing us to focus on doing our job until we could get back to them.

I want to recognize, through this story, the service of my family members. Each paid some and some paid all. It was an honor to follow in their footsteps.

Let us never forget the cost that has been paid for the freedoms we enjoy. And let us keep their stories alive so the next generation can understand the true cost of freedom.

PREFACE

Benjamin Franklin once wrote that "if you want to be remembered longer than thirty minutes after you're dead, you should either do something worth writing about or you should write something worth reading about." It is my intention, with this book, to do the latter by telling a story of a generation that saved the world.

I truly believe that in our nation's history, there were three major events that not only changed the course of history but changed the course of mankind. The first was the American Revolution. When men, begging to be free and independent, risk everything they had or ever hoped to have to break from the restraints of the most powerful nation on earth. They faced countless uncertainties, and against all odds, they committed to make the sacrifices so they and every generation who would follow could be free and independent from any other country. They had a dream and understood that to fulfill that dream, it would require them to dedicate all their efforts to a cause that was greater than any of them. We cannot truly understand their struggle, fear, or uncertainty they faced when they started their quest because the results of their effort is known and has been well documented.

The second generation that would be tested would be those men and women of the mid-nineteenth century. Their calling would test the very foundation of the republic to see if it could withstand descent from within itself. Our country was made up of several states independent from each other but bound by the common belief granted in our constitution. This would be America's darkest moment as well as its brightest moment. A time that would be mired by tragedy, triumph, and suffering. It was a time when an injustice, for too many decades had been ignored, would be challenged and won. A time when a nation and a generation once and for all to honor a commitment that was secured in the words that was written in the declaration of independence. Words declaring that "all men have been created equal in the eyes of God" were not just words but now a reality. After the struggles of this great civil war, our country would rise to be stronger, more united, and more productive than any time leading up to the war. It would also be the time when the constitution would be tested to ensure that the safe and orderly transfer of power could take place with the assignation of President Lincoln.

Finally, I believe those who answered the third call and fulfilled their destiny in the world were the men and women who fought World War II. This was a generation that would suffer through the hardship of a great depression. They did not know this at the time, but that struggle they face would be the foundation they would need to meet the greater challenge of World War II. My decision to write this book comes from the compelling need I have had to tell their story through the life of a common family. Even though this story is about one family from Iowa, it is the similar story of millions of families who served during this time. These men and women understood, like the two generations before them, that their calling was bigger than themselves, and the outcome would alter the history of mankind.

I dedicate this book to my father, Donald Raymond Vaughn, and mother, Lavaun Martha Mitchell Vaughn, whom the inspiration as well as the story comes from. They were simple hard working young adults who were beginning their lives as one family when this war broke out. Like so many young couples, they were looking forward to the future away from the depression where they could live, prosper, and begin their lives as a married couple. They wanted to live their life in Iowa, raise their family, work, and contribute back to the community they called home. But their generation would set aside their personal goals and went without question to war. Not because they wanted to, not for the glory of the fight but because their generation understood that they had an obligation to rid the world of the hatred of a madman. They sacrifice greatly at home and abroad. Their sacrifices could not just be measured in the cost of waging a world war, but the greater cost was the millions of lives that were lost to secure the nations from the stranglehold they were under.

All three generations shared a single bond. The results were unknown to them at the time they began their battle, but they knew they had to endure the hardship, pay the cost, and make the sacrifice because the results of their calling was greater than themselves. We cannot duplicate their effort, dedicate, or even write enough to repay them for the cost they bore. But we can keep alive the gifts they gave us because of their efforts and promises they made to us. We can honor them by telling their stories and share them with all who are willing to listen or read. It is my hope that this story is read by a million readers, not because of the money but because we need to remember and understand the selfless sacrifice of the men and women who made up the greatest generation of the twentieth century.

Mom and Dad

Chapter 1

JUST GETTING STARTED

It was early morning as the sun pushed its way into the bedroom. The crystal design on the window revealed the evidence of a heavy frost and the gentle reminder that winter would soon be here. It was the weekend, and Jim knew there was no need to get up, but he also knew he could not stay in bed without waking his wife, Anna. He gently pushed back the covers and slid out of bed. As his foot touched the floor, he quickly drew it back, discovering that the coldness of the morning had made its way into the old house and the wooden floors.

Jim stepped out of bed thinking they might need to get a throw rug before winter set in, and this became an everyday event. But for now, he needed to head down to the basement and shovel some coal into the furnace to raise the temperature before Anna got up. Jim walked over to the chair by the window and found his shirt, coveralls, and socks right where he had left them the night before. He quickly dressed and headed to the kitchen to put on a pot of coffee before he went outside to attend to getting some heat into the house. He tried to be as quiet as he could, but the inner makings of the coffee pot fell out and hit the floor with a clang. Jim waited a minute to hear any stirring coming from the bedroom before he bent down and picked it up. He filled the pot with water, added four scoops of freshly ground coffee, and lit the stove. He set the pot over the fire and headed to the coat rack by the back door. He slipped on his boots and was reaching for his coat when he heard Anna. She too had discovered the temperature of the floor.

"Jim, what do you have the furnace set on?"

Jim answered, "I am heading outside right now to get some coal in the furnace and some heat in the house. I have the coffee on, so why don't you just stay in bed. I will come into the bedroom and let you know once I can get some heat in here."

Anna replied, "If you do, I am thinking we won't be getting up."

Jim laughed and said, "Well, it is Saturday, and we haven't got anything planned for the day, do we?"

"Jim, how could you forget? Don't you remember you told Dad you would help him fix the leak in his roof today?" she asked.

"No, I guess I forgot. The thought of having you all to myself for a day can make a man forget a lot of things."

"Oh, Jim, just get some heat in the house, and I will start breakfast." As Jim went out the back door, Anna put on her bathrobe and went to the front door. She reached into the metal container sitting on the porch to get the order she had left for the milkman the night before. The order was correct: two bottles of milk, a carton of cottage cheese, and one bottle of heavy cream. Now Anna didn't normally buy cream because of the expense, but she would need it to make a whipping cream for the pumpkin pies she was baking for Thanksgiving at her parent's house this Thursday. Anna opened her new refrigerator and thought how nice it was that she no longer had to mess with ice to keep the food cold. She placed the milk, cottage cheese, and cream on the shelves and took out the carton of eggs along with the slab of bacon. Jim usually didn't have time during the week for a good breakfast, as he would rather sleep a little longer than mess with eating. So this morning, Anna wanted to fix him a hearty one, especially if he was going to be outside working on her father's roof.

Anna grabbed a couple of potatoes and an onion from the pantry and put some lard into the iron skillet. She sliced the potatoes into the pan then started chopping the onion for flavor. As she wiped away tears, she remembered what her mom had told her. "Put the onion in the regenerator overnight, and then you won't cry when you chop them." She added salt and pepper and then lit the stove. She lit the other burner and set another iron skillet over the flame. She sliced the bacon and eased it into the pan. With both burners now on high, she turned and opened the bread box only to discover they had just one slice left, and that was the heel, which Jim didn't care for. Anna put the bread back into the box and decided she would make a stack of pancakes instead.

As Anna was beating the flour for the pancakes, she reached over and turned the radio on to listen to some music. She knew when Jim came in, he would want to listen to the news; but for now, a little Jimmy Dorsey was in order.

Anna loved music, and she loved to dance and roller skate, which is where she first met Jim. It was 1939, and she was skating with her best friend Hazel Mitchell, whom she worked with as an operator at the local telephone company. She noticed Jim out on the skating rink and how well he skated. Jim was a little over six feet tall and slim with broad shoulders. He had jet black hair that was parted on one side and combed back. Anna asked Hazel if she knew who he was, and she said that she knew of him. He was from a small town about twenty miles away and had graduated in 1938 just like they did. He worked as a salesman for a tobacco company, and he worked part-time on the weekend at the skating rink. As they were talking, a progressive skate started for the men. Now a progressive skate is when the a guy asks any gal in the rink to skate with him. As they are skating, a whistle blows, and the guy moves up to the next girl in front of him. This goes on until the music stops.

Jim came over to Anna, introduced himself, and asked if she would like to skate with him. Anna's first thought was to say yes, but she didn't think it would be proper since they had not been formally introduced, and she certainly didn't want to give the wrong impression. So she said, "Thank you, but no." Jim said, "Well, maybe another day" and skated away. Hazel asked Anna what she was doing, and she said, "I will ask him when it is girls' choice."

Anna watched Jim and was impressed with how well he skated and especially his ability to skate with the rhythm of the music. Hazel told Anna that his last name was McManis and that his father was one of the local barbers down on Church Street.

Finally, it was the girls' choice, so Anna skated over to where Jim was standing, talking with some other boys. She tapped Jim on the shoulder and said, "Would you like to skate?

Jim looked at her and said, "Sorry, I can't. I have been asked by another gal to save this one for her."

Well, Anna was furious, thinking what a cocky person he was and just who did he think he was, some sort of ladies' man? "Don't Irish men have any manners?" she mumbled as she skated away.

Anna and Jim would see each other many more evenings at the skating rink, and they eventually had their progressive skate. Their weekends centered on these moments together at the skating rink, and finally on July 4, 1941, they were married. Anna was a very petite gal only weighing ninety-nine pounds. Her hair was dark brown, and she wore it to her shoulders where it flipped under just a little bit. Her hair was very fine, almost like silk, and it glistened in the sunlight and blew softly if caught by the wind. Her eyes were so blue it put the sky to shame, and her skin was fair and soft. She was the most beautiful gal Jim had ever seen, and he knew she was going to be his wife the first time he saw her. It took Anna a few more times, however, before she came to the same conclusion.

* * * *

Anna turned to the door as Jim opened it and walked in announcing that it wouldn't be too long now before they would have some heat in their old house. He heard the sizzling of the bacon and caught the aroma of the fried potatoes cooking as he reached for a cup and filled it with coffee. Jim walked over to the radio and asked Anna if she would mind if he changed the radio station.

Anna said, "Just as soon as this song is over. You have a few more minutes before the morning news will be on anyway, so why don't you sit down and enjoy the music?"

Jim said, "Do you even know the name of this song?"

Anna answered, "Of course. It's a new song by Tex Beneke called *'Chattanooga Choo-Choo.'* You might know that if you didn't spend so much of your time listening to the news."

Jim asked Anna if she would like to go to the skating rink tonight if they got done early enough at her parents' house.

"Maybe, we will have to see," she replied. "I hear they raised the price to a dime per person. Imagine a dime just to go around in circles on wooden wheels," Anna protested.

"Oh, Anna, you know you love to skate, and besides, I enjoy watching your back side as you go around that rink."

"Jim, you're terrible! Is that all you think about?"

Jim laughed and said, "Not always, but when you're skating."

Anna chuckled and told Jim to go wash his hands as she was frying up his eggs. Breakfast would be ready soon.

Before Jim sat down, he changed the channel on the radio just in time to listen to a news account of the German General Rommel and the Axis Army who were having their way against the Fifth South African Brigade. According to the news account, after several days of tank battles around Tobruk, Rommel's tanks had pushed to cut off the supply lines to the British in an operation that would later be called "the dash for the wire." Things were not going well in Africa, and most of Europe was now under German rule. It seemed every news story was about the Germans success and providing a reason this war would eventually come to America. Anna listened and asked Jim if he thought President Roosevelt would keep his word and stay out of this fight.

Jim looked over at Anna and said, "I am not sure he has many options with what's going on. It appears that this nut, Hitler, is intent on taking over all of Europe, and I think at some point those boys over there are going to need our help."

Jim looked over and saw how upset this news was to Anna, so he reached over and tuned the radio to another channel finding the show *Stars over Hollywood*. It was a Saturday morning comedy show that often featured stars who showed up in their pajamas because it started so early in the morning on the west coast. Jim looked at Anna and saw she was deep in thought about the future and said, "Well, there is nothing we can do about what is going on, and worrying about what might be isn't going to change our plans. So let's just enjoy this great breakfast you've made and get ready to go over to your parents. Anna, are we out of bread?"

Anna replied, "Any that you would eat."

After breakfast, Jim went out on the front porch to enjoy his pipe, while Anna cleaned up the kitchen. As Jim lit his pipe, he looked out to watch his neighbors who were raking their yards and piling up the last reminder of fall. They lived in a quite small rural community in the southeastern corner of Iowa. The people there were hardworking, honest folks who believed in God, family, and each other. During bad times, they all pulled together and helped out everyone in the community. And just like everywhere else in the country, they had been through some bad times the last few years.

Being a small community, everyone knew everyone, and everyone knew your business. Sharing their phones on party lines, one could easily pick up a receiver and listen in on a conversation if they wanted, and many times did. Jim always was complaining to Anna about Mable, an old widow who lived across the street and shared their line, asking if she ever did anything else but listen in or gossip on the phone.

Jim sat in the swing and watched the children in the neighborhood as they were running through and jumping in those same leaves their fathers were trying to gather. Through their laughter, he could hear the occasional father scolding them for the extra work they were causing. In the air, you could smell the burning leaves and feel the crispness of the fall. Jim loved this time of year when the days were warm and the evenings cold enough to enjoy a sweater or a light jacket. A small fire in the fireplace was in order on some nights as he and Anna sat on the couch either reading the paper, talking, or just cuddling like newlyweds often do. They would just hold each other as they listened to the radio, and Anna, who often sang along, impressed Jim with her knowing all the words to the song.

Jim began thinking about his new life with Anna and how perfect it was. He wondered how war would alter their plans when it finally came. Jim had just started a new job at the local dairy getting his own route. He was so grateful to have work. Many of the men his age were still struggling to find steady employment as the country was coming out of the terrible times of the depression. The Depression years were hard on so many, and his family wasn't spared. Jim's father had a hard time at the barbershop he owned. Being Irish, there were a lot who wouldn't come to him, and the customers he had didn't come as often because of the economic times they were going through. He knew, compared to so many, they were actually lucky; at least they always had some food to eat and a place to stay. Now with the Depression easing, he was getting started on a great job that was paying him twenty dollars a week. The 1935 Plymouth he drove was paid for and, knock on wood, was running well.

Jim had an agreement with Old Doc Wagner, the local family doctor who was the owner of the house, to pay nineteen dollars a month rent as long as he would take care of all the maintenance including the yard, the barn, and the old coal furnace which required a lot of Jim's attention, at least in the winter. Doc Wagner had put city water in the house right before he rented it to Jim, which meant no outhouse or hauling water from the well out back. It was something Anna's parents hadn't done yet, but Anna knew her mom, and it wasn't going to be long before her dad would be doing the same.

Anna worked part-time about twenty hours a week as a telephone operator, which was a very good job that paid her seventeen cents an hour. Jim and Anna had been talking about starting their family now that he had steady work. But with the uncertainty of the times, they both knew this wasn't the time to make changes.

Jim worried, if war did come, how involved would this country become? Would he be expected to join like Anna's father did in World War I? What about Anna? Could she afford to stay in the house on what she made as a telephone operator and what he could send home? Might she have to move in with her parents?

Jim stopped and reminded himself of the advice he had earlier given Anna and changed his thoughts to the day. He looked up into the sky to see there wasn't a cloud to be found. He thought of something his mother always said. "Son," she would say, "if there is enough blue in the sky to make a pair of jeans, then it isn't going to rain today." He laughed and said, "Well, Mom, I guess we can make a lot of jeans today."

He heard the distant whistle of the Burlington Northern train and looked at his watch. Yep, late as always; it was ten minutes after nine. There was a strong breeze blowing in from the north, and as it crossed the river, it picked up a chill which told him that, even though there were no clouds in the sky, the temperature probably wasn't going to get much above fifty today.

He yelled into Anna that she would probably need more than just a sweater when they went over to her parents' house.

Anna asked how much longer he would be as the morning was getting late and if they were going to get over to her parents' house, fix the roof, and get back in time to go skating, he might want to put a rush in his pipe enjoyment.

Jim answered, "I can be ready in about ten minutes, just need to wash up and shave."

Anna said she was going to go get ready and fix her hair, and she should be ready in about a half an hour. "Jim, do you want to take the trolley or drive the car?"

"Let's take the car. I don't want you to be standing around in the cold waiting on the trolley when it's time to go."

"Oh, I don't mind," Anna replied. "But if you would prefer to drive, I am fine with that. Do you have enough gas to last until Thursday when you get paid?"

Jim answered, "I have enough gas to last a couple of weeks. Remember I only have to drive to work and home now that I have the milk truck to do my deliveries."

"Okay," Anna answered, "then why don't you get ready and get the car out of the barn and bring it around front. I should be ready by then."

It was a short drive over to Anna's parents' house, which was located on the other side of the river by the Lowenberg bakery. Anna looked out the window as Jim drove and commented on how pretty this fall was and how she hated to see all the leaves on the ground. "I believe the fall leaves were more colorful than they had been in previous years," she said.

"I think you're right," Jim replied. "They say the color and the brightness has something to do with the moisture, and it predicts how much snow we will have this winter. So if what they say is true, we are in for a lot of snow this winter."

Anna laughed and said, "I don't put a lot of trust in those old wives' tales. Kind of like that story your mom says about the blue sky."

As they were driving over the bridge, Anna saw the roof of the bakery, so she rolled down the window just enough to allow the aroma of the freshly baked bread to come into the car.

"Don't you just love the smell from the bakery Jim?" she exclaimed. "Yes, it really smells good, which reminds me will we need to stop at the grocery store and pick up a loaf before we go home today? Can you think of anything else we will need before pay day?" Jim asked.

"Well, if we can afford it, I need some lard, sugar, and flour to make pie crust, and I could make a loaf or two of bread," Anna replied.

"Maybe you could make some cinnamon rolls for the morning so I could grab one with my morning coffee as I head out the door," Jim suggested.

Anna said, "That would be fine. If I am already making bread, making cinnamon rolls isn't any more work. But we will need to add cinnamon to the list."

"Well," Jim said, "in that case, I think I have enough money in my pocket to handle those few items."

"Will that leave us enough to go skating?" Anna inquired.

"Yes, we can even get some popcorn and split a soda if we want. That is, of course, if we get done with the roof in time. You know how your father likes to talk. Maybe we should stop at the store before we get over there," Jim commented.

Anna agreed that would probably be a good idea. Jim reminded Anna that her parents would expect them to stay for super.

"I know. We will eat, and when we are done, I will help Mom with the dishes. You can sit and talk with Dad for a little bit and maybe we can get out in time so we can go. I will tell them we are going skating after dinner. They were young and newlyweds once. I am sure they will understand."

Jim chuckled and said, "I hope so, but calling them newlyweds, well, that was a long time ago."

"Jim," Anna protested, "you're impossible sometimes. You know what I meant."

They stopped at Bob's Market, which was only about one block from where Anna's parents lived, and got the items they needed. As they were turning the corner to her parents' house, Anna saw the family dog sitting in the yard. "Oh, look at Queenie waiting as if she knew I was coming."

"Probably does," Jim answered. Queenie was a small black-and-white terrier that followed Anna home from school one day in 1935. It was just a small puppy that couldn't have been any older than four months. Anna tried to ignore the dog, as she didn't think her parents would be none too happy with another mouth to feed. But to her surprise, when she walked outside to go to school the next morning, out from under the porch came Queenie wagging her tail and looking up at her. Anna tried to ignore the pup as she followed along to school. The pup would wait outside for school to end and then followed her home again. She slipped the dog table scraps and finally told her mom and dad about the dog and what had happened. Her father said, "Whoever had the dog probably couldn't afford to keep her, and well, the dog knew a sucker with a big heart when she saw one and followed you home."

"So I can keep her?" Anna asked.

"Yes, but just remember she's your dog, and you're responsible for her," her father replied.

* * *

The dog's head popped up, and her tail started wagging as Jim and Anna pulled into the driveway. Both the dog and Craig, Anna's father, came walking to the car. As Anna stepped out, she gave her dad a hug, patted the dog on the head, and asked, "Where's Mom?"

"Oh, you know your mom. She is probably making a fuss over something in the kitchen." Craig yelled into the house, "Mary, the kids are here."

Just about then, Anna heard the screen door slam as her mother came out on the porch. She was wiping her hands on her apron and then waved. "Anna, come in the kitchen. I have something to show you."

"Okay, Mom," Anna replied as she walked to the house. She then turned and said, "I will leave you two alone to get to that roof. Now remember, Jim, we have a date later on tonight, so don't dally." She blew him a kiss.

Craig smiled and asked, "Got plans tonight?"

"Yes," Jim said, "I told Anna we would go to the skating rink tonight if we got everything done we needed to do today, and it wasn't too late."

"Oh, I don't think it will take long to put a few shingles on the roof," answered Craig.

Craig went on to say, "Now her mother could be another matter. She apparently doesn't think you're getting enough to eat, so she has planned a big supper."

The men went to the roof, and Anna went into the kitchen to join her mom.

"What is it that you want to show me, Mom?" Anna asked.

"This hat your father bought me. Can you believe he bought this hat? And to make the matter worse he wants me to wear it to church next Sunday!"

Anna laughed and said, "Well, it sure will look better on you than on me."

"That isn't a bit funny, Anna. What is with the net over my face? Is he trying to tell me something?"

"Oh, Mom, you know Dad. He just saw something pretty and thought it would look good on you."

"Well, I can assure," Mary insisted, "that neither you nor anyone else will be seeing me wearing this hat to church this Sunday or any other Sunday that will follow. I can't believe any decent woman would wear such a thing."

Anna put on an apron and asked how she could help.

"You can start by giving me a hand with those potatoes. I need to get them on the stove and boiling. I will finish dressing the pheasants your father shot this morning. It shouldn't be long, and you can take the mincemeat pie out of the oven. Jim does like mincemeat, doesn't he?"

Anna answered, "Well, Mom, I'm not sure, but I haven't found anything he won't eat yet, so I would imagine the pie will be just fine."

Mary asked, "Would you like a cup of coffee?"

"Thanks, Mom, I think I would, "Anna replied.

"I just made a fresh pot, so help yourself. It's on the stove, and if you don't mind, can you freshen up my cup?' Mary asked.

Jim walked around back of the house to the tool shed to get the tar, roofing nails, and shingles. Craig was bringing the ladder around from the garage so they could get to the roof. The house was built in May of 1923. It was a two-story three-bedroom house that was built on a stone foundation with a basement. It had a modest living room with a red stone fireplace, a dark oak wooden mantel, a more formal dining room, and a large kitchen. Craig loved to cook, so he insisted that the kitchen be roomy and that it be a place for others to gather. As he always said, "If you want to find the crowd, find the food."

There was a staircase with stained oak railing that led up to the bedrooms, and, of course, the bathroom was outside. At the bottom of the staircase was a wooden coat rack that had been in the Middleton family for over one hundred years. Middleton was Anna's maiden name. There was a large covered front porch with a swing attached to the ceiling for those evening sessions of doing nothing but swinging, smoking, and thinking. Going out from the kitchen, you walked to the enclosed mudroom. Built in the floor was a door that took you to the storm cellar in the basement, a place to go when those crazy Iowa spring storms came.

Craig and Mary lived comfortably on the wages Craig earned as a rural letter carrier for the post office. Mary did not work outside of the home. They had raised two children: their daughter Anna and a son named Arthur, who just graduated from high school and was still living at home. Arthur worked at the local John Deere plant and was away in Moline, Illinois, learning about the new Model L series that was scheduled to start being built at their plant.

Art was a very bright young man. and even at the age of nineteen, his boss sent him over to Moline to attend the meetings on the newest products being built by their company and to listen in on the discussion of the direction the company would take if war should break out. Art stood about five feet eight and probably didn't weigh more than one hundred and twenty pounds. He wasn't overly muscular, but he was very scrappy as many of his fellow classmates found out when they tried to bully him or pull one over on him. Many times Art would come home with a black eye always proclaiming to his worried mom, "You should see the other guy."

This was a good Christian family who believed that you went to church every Sunday, unless you were not able to get out of bed. You looked after each other, and you cared for those in need. They were private people in that they didn't take much to gossip or spend a lot of time fussing over what someone else had or thought. Well, maybe Mary did when it came to hats that Craig bought her to wear to church.

Craig was a veteran of the Mexican Border war as a member of the Iowa National Guard, and he enlisted and served in the army during World War I. He believed in service, and he believed that each person had an obligation to give back something for the freedoms they enjoyed. If war broke out, there was no doubt he would enlist again. The only question was, at his age, what branch of service would take him and to do what?

* * * *

Craig and Jim had just finished the roof, and as they were climbing down, they heard Mary come out on the porch to inform them it was time to come in and wash up for supper.

The dinner conversations covered the normal talk about family, work, Thanksgiving and eventually moved to politics and the world events. Craig started inquiring what Jim felt was going on with the Japanese and what they were up to.

"Well, do you think they have any intentions of sitting down and talking with us about their plans?" Jim asked."

"I think it is inevitable they will try to start something soon," answered Craig.

Jim, realizing how upsetting these conversations were for Anna, tried the best he could to keep his answers short and very general so as not to encourage additional comments or questions.

Craig stated his disappointment that the Germans were back to their old tricks, saying, "Well, it looks like we might have to go back over there and kick their butt just like we did a few years back."

"Oh, Craig, must we have this conversation at the table?" Mary asked.

Finally, the one question came that Jim was hoping to avoid.

"So have you given any thought as to what you will do if the United States enters this war?" Craig asked.

Luckily for Jim, he didn't have to answer that question because they were interrupted by a knock on the door. As they all turned to look, there was Arthur walking in, apparently getting home early from Moline.

"Art, when did you get in, and why didn't you call?" Mary asked

"Oh, Mom, it was a nice day, and I enjoyed the walk from the train station. I figured you would be sitting down to supper, and Sis and Jim would be over here. I mean, we all have eaten Anna's cooking."

"Oh, Art, how you tease your sister," Jim said. "She is a very good cook, and I think I have even gained a few pounds since we got married."

"Oh yes, you're a regular fat guy," Art said.

"Have you had your supper?" Mary asked, "Why don't you pull up a chair and sit down while I fix you a plate."

"It's okay, Mom. I grabbed something downtown, so sit down and eat while the food was hot. I can get a cup from the kitchen."

Art pulled out a chair, sat down, lit up a cigarette, and said, "Dad, I am sorry I wasn't here to help you with the roof, but I wasn't sure how long I was going to be in Moline."

"No big deal. Jim came over, and it only took us about an hour or so," Craig replied.

"Anyone want some coffee?" Anna asked as she got up and went to the kitchen.

"Bring the pot," Art said, "I am sure we would all like a refill if you're pouring." "So," Art started on Anna, "any baby news, Sis?"

Anna blushed and said, "Well, if there is, you will be the third or maybe the forth person to find out."

Mary cut a slice of pie for each person and served it with the coffee.

"Jim, you do like mincemeat pie, don't you?" she asked.

"Oh yes, I remember times when that pie would be our evening meal," Jim replied.

As Art cut into his pie, he started talking about the new tractor model they were making and how big it was going to be for the company.

He went on to say that much of the conversations were centered on the role John Deere could play in the manufacturing of equipment for the Department of Defense if war broke out.

Jim looked over to see Anna and her mother clearing the table. Craig and Art grabbed their coffee and headed to the living room. Art continued on, saying he didn't see how Roosevelt was going to keep his campaign promise and stay out of this war with the pressure being applied by England and the other European countries.

"I know the president ran his last election campaign on a policy of staying neutral, but how long and at what cost can we stay out of this fight?" Art asked. "We are Americans. We love a good fight, and I don't know about you, but I am ready to go kick some butt."

"Don't be in such a hurry," Craig said. "If it starts, you will get your fill soon enough. That, I am sure."

Art went on saying, "The damn Germans seem hell bent for leather to occupy all of Europe, and I don't trust the Japanese at all. They are up to something, and if they team up with Germany, the world could be in real trouble."

Jim sat and listened to the conversation and then said, "Well, we can't change what will be, so we had better take care of now, hope for the best, and be ready if war comes."

"My god, my sister married a philosopher," Art said with a laugh.

Jim laughed and said, "Well, I am not sure about that. But I do know no one is going to be asking my opinion. So I know I am not going to have any say in the matter."

"What are your thoughts on the war?" asked Art.

"Politics belongs to those who know a lot more than I do," Jim replied.

"But what are your plans if war breaks out?" asked Craig.

"Well, I guess that will depend on the options I have," Jim replied, realizing what he had just said could be taken wrong. Especially with the strong belief that this family had for service, he quickly added, "I probably will look into joining the navy."

"That is what I am going to do," said Craig. "Art and I are thinking we would enlist and hopefully serve together. Maybe get an assignment to a ship in the Atlantic." Craig blew out smoke from his cigarette and said, "One war in the army filled with dirt, trenches, lousy food, walking, and no sleep was enough for me."

Jim reached into his pocket to find his pipe and tobacco as Art stood up and walked into the kitchen. He grabbed Anna around the waist, giving her a little kiss on the check and said. "So, Sis, need some help with the dishes?"

"Sure," said Anna. "Getting bored with the men?" "Nope, just thought I would help, but if you don't want—"

Anna interrupted and said, "No, that's fine. I like listening to your babble."

Craig reached over to the radio and asked Jim if he would rather listen to the Grand Ole Opry or to the Texaco Star Theater with Fred Allen? Jim didn't have to think long. He wasn't a fan of hillbilly music, so he said, "I am fine with the Texaco Star Theater if it is good for you."

Jim looked into the kitchen and heard Anna and her brother talking and laughing. He realized they would be staying late and that skating would have to come another evening. Jim didn't mind. He understood that this time his wife spent with her brother and family was more important than an evening of skating. They had the car and had already stopped at the grocery store, so with all the uncertainty in the world, they could go skating another time. Jim eased back into the big oversized chair and re lit his pipe. As he blew out a few puffs of smoke, he listened to the radio and glanced at Craig who was catching a quick nap in his favorite chair.

Chapter 2

A DAY THAT LIVES IN INFAMY

It was a typical Iowa Sunday morning in December when Jim woke and headed out the door. He was meeting Art over at the Coffee Cup Cafe, and the two of them were going hunting before they headed to Craig's for Sunday dinner. The weather was dry with the skies overcast and the temperatures just hovering around the freezing mark. There was a slight breeze blowing just out of the north, which made it seem even colder than the thermometer said. You could sense that snow would be coming soon, but for now, other than an occasional flurry, there was no snow on the ground.

Jim thought about those who look forward to having snow for Christmas and how they wouldn't be disappointed this year. He recalled the fall colors and his earlier prediction for the upcoming winter and thought how he could kid Anna who was a disbeliever in old wives' tales.

It wasn't the best weather for hunting quail because with temperatures around freezing, they would be more apt to sit and run along the ground instead of taking flight. Jim thought to himself these are the days he wished he had a good bird dog.

He was just getting a refill on his coffee when he saw Art walk through the door.

"Good morning, Jim," Art called out.

"Good morning. Need a cup of coffee before we head out?" Jim asked. Jim caught the eye of his waitress, and she brought over another cup for Art and topped off Jim's.

"Need to see a breakfast menu?" asked the waitress.

"No, thank you, just coffee for me. Mom was already up when I came into the kitchen and had fixed toast and oatmeal. I sometimes wonder if she ever sleeps."

"Do you want to go over to old man Gustafson's farm and walk his cornfield?" Art asked.

"Yes, I asked him yesterday if it would be all right if we stopped over today. He said he saw a few coveys when he was out moving the cows over to another field."

"It is going to be hard to get them to fly with this weather," Jim said. "So I was thinking I could walk in front and try to stir them up if you promise not to shoot me."

Art chuckled and said, "You don't need to worry about that. You get them flying. I have Dad's new Browning 20 gauge shotgun, so if we can get them to fly, it will knock them down."

Both men finished their coffee, and Jim laid a quarter on the table and waved goodbye to the waitress. You could hear the bell above the door chime as Art opened it and walked out. As they headed for the car, a gentle snow started to fall. The flakes were big, and instead of falling from the sky, they floated as if they were little gliders catching the wind, allowing the breeze to move them around as if they were dancing to a tune bouncing with each note. The flakes were too big to amount for much other to provide a dusting to mother earth.

Art said to Jim, "I think it has either gotten colder, or the sight of the snow makes it seem that way." Jim brushed the snow off the windshield and started the car. They headed out of town and turned onto old highway 34. The farm was about thirteen miles out, and as they drove, you could see that many of the farmers had not done any cultivating of their fields this year. Cornstalks, standing about knee high, could be seen all the way to the tree line.

"All these corn stalks should make for some good cover for the animals," Art said.

"Well, we will see," said Jim. "If nothing else, the deer will not starve this winter."

They pulled into the long drive and drove through the grove to the farmhouse where they parked the car. Both Jim and Art got out, leaving their guns behind in the trunk, and walked up to let Mr. Gustafson know they were there and that they would be heading to the field.

As they stepped up onto the porch, Mr. Gustafson opened the door and invited them to come in. Jim declined saying they wanted to get to the field as they were on a timetable and had to get back for dinner. Mr. Gustafson reminded them that he had cows out in the field and hoped they would not mistake them for any deer. He then went on and told a story about another farmer about six miles away who found two of his cows shot by hunters. They would be the only ones in the field hunting, as he had not given permission to anyone else. He extended an invitation to stop in when they were done to warm themselves and have coffee before heading back into town. Jim, realizing Mr. Gustafson and Art had not met, said, "Tom, I apologized for being so rude. This is my wife's brother Art. Art, this is Tom Gustafson."

Art tipped his hat and said, "Nice to meet you, Mr. Gustafson." They excused themselves and headed to the car to get their guns.

As they walked to the field, each man placed a few shells in his pocket, but none in the shotguns. As they opened the gate, they entered the field and loaded their guns. Jim and Art each took a row and started a slow steady walk down the path. With each step, you could hear the crunch of the frozen ground as it gave way to the weight of their boots. The snow had stopped, but the wind had picked up, and Jim looked to the trees to see which way the wind was blowing. He knew if they kicked up quail, that would be the direction they would fly. So he wanted to check what was out in front of him before he fired his gun. Just then, Art stepped in the middle of a covey of birds, and the sound of their wings taking flight not only startled them both, but instead of shooting, Art yelled, "There they go."

Jim got both barrels off, but only one bird fell. Jim started laughing and said to Art, "Nice shot."

Art answered, "They scared the hell out of me, and by the time I recovered, the only thing I could do was yell."

"Well, that shotgun may have a big pattern when you fire, but I think if you're going to hit anything, you will need to pull the trigger because yelling at them didn't work."

"Yes, very funny. They got me once, but now that I know they are sitting, it won't happen again."

The sun was brightly shining now it had finally burned its way through the overcast gray winter sky. Jim glanced up and said, "We had better call it a day and start heading for home."

It turned out to be a good day to hunt. They had each shot three quail and a couple of rabbits. They knew by the time they field dressed the game and got home, it would be time to wash up and head over to

Craig's for the afternoon. They stopped by the house to say thank-you and offer Mr. Gustafson the rabbits. They declined his invite for coffee, saying they had stayed longer than they should have but would next time. Tom thanked them for the rabbits but said he had plenty and knew where he could get more if he needed.

As Art and Jim walked to the car, Art said, "I would think a guy could get kind of lonely out here, especially in the winter when folks didn't get around that much."

Tom agreed, saying, "I think it takes a special kind of folk to be a farmer, and I know I am not one of them."

They got to the car, broke the guns down, and laid them in the backseat. Jim started up the engine, turned the wheel of the car, and headed back through the grove down the driveway and out to the highway.

Art said that Mom would more than likely want to go out and find a Christmas tree today after dinner.

"Well, we are right here should we turn around and go back and ask Mr. Gustafson?" Jim asked.

"I see this is your first Christmas with Anna," said Art. "You cut down any Christmas tree without her being there. Well, let me just say it could make for a very unpleasant day."

Jim acknowledged the comment and kept driving.

Art continued, "I remember every Christmas when we were young. Dad would take us out into the woods, and we would find and cut down a tree. Every year, it was the same. The tree was too small, but Dad would say it would do and over our objections cut it down anyway. As soon as he got the tree into the house, we realized the ones we had picked would have never made it through the door, and they would have been taller than the ceiling."

Jim laughed and said, "Yes, things look different when you're out in the open."

Art paused, looked out the window and said, "Can you imagine the sight of the ocean from the deck of a ship? I can't imagine anything could look larger than that."

Jim glanced over at Art and realized that the events of the world were more troubling to him than he was letting on. He was tough on the outside, but inside, he was like everyone else unsure of tomorrow and maybe just a little scared of what was to come.

Jim dropped Art off at the cafe and headed home. He pulled into the drive, removed the game and his shotgun from the seat, and came inside announcing his entrance to Anna.

"Honey, I am home. I am going to put the game I shot in the sink and clean the shotgun. What time did you tell your parents we would be over?"

"I said around eleven. Mom wants to eat early so we can go pick out this year's Christmas tree. Jim, make sure you put a little salt in the sink with the water so the game can soak for a while. I take it you and Art had fun?" Anna asked.

"Yes, I first thought Art was the bird dog instead of a hunter, but I will tell that story later at the dinner table."

"Oh, Jim, now don't be embarrassing Art. He thinks a lot of you." "Don't worry. I won't He is a good guy."

Jim took out the cleaning supplies and broke down his shotgun so he could clean it. He carefully cleaned each piece and then oiled them to prevent any rust or unnecessary wear on any of the parts. When he was done, he reassembled the shotgun and placed it in the hall closet so it would be ready the next time he goes hunting. He removed all his shells he had in his coat pocket and placed them in an old cigar box. His father taught Jim "that you always keep your ammo close, but never store it in the gun unless you're ready to use it."

As Jim headed to the bathroom, he remembered what Anna said about salt and poured a little in the sink. Anna was just stepping out of the bathtub as Jim entered. Jim looked at Anna as she was drying herself off and asked, "How much time do we have before we have to leave?"

"Oh, Jim, just go shave and do something with your hair. I don't want to be late."

It was 10:00 a.m. Central time on Sunday, December 7, 1941, and there was no way for Jim, Anna, or anyone to know that off the coast of Oahu in the Hawaiian islands laid a Japanese fleet who were making their final preparations to attack the United States Naval base at Pearl Harbor.

Art and Craig were sitting on the front porch, and Queenie was lying on the steps when Jim pulled in the driveway. Craig was still in the clothes he had worn to church swinging in the big porch swing and smoking a cigarette. Anna looked at her father and said to Jim, "I bet Mom didn't wear that hat Dad gave her." There was another young lady sitting beside Art, and Anna thought that her brother finally had gotten enough nerve to bring his girlfriend over to the house.

"Jim, did you know Art was bringing a guest for dinner today?"

Jim looked to the porch and said, "He didn't say anything about it to me."

As they approached the porch, Art stood up and said hello. "Anna, Jim, I would like you to meet my girlfriend Sara, Sara Shoemaker."

"Nice to meet you, Sara, and welcome," said Anna as she reached out to take Sara's hand.

"Shoemaker, are you the daughter of Doc Shoemaker, the veterinarian who lives by the Methodist church?" inquired Jim.

"Well, yes," said Sara "he is that Shoemaker, and we do live there. Do you know my father?"

"Not really, but I have seen him a few times when he was in my father's barbershop. Don't think he was a regular, but Dad spoke of him kindly."

"What is your father's name," asked Sara.

"Patrick Shane McManis," answered Jim.

"Oh yes, my father has spoken of him," he said. "There were not many Irish men he cared for, but your father was the exception to that rule."

"Well, Dad is Irish and very proud of that fact, but if you ask, he will tell you he is an American first."

"I would imagine that is the reason Dad speaks so kindly of him," Sara concluded.

Craig stood up and said, "Well, I think we should all go in. There is no need to catch the death of pneumonia by not having enough brains to know when it's time to get out of the cold."

It was a little past eleven when they sat down at the table. Craig had turned on the radio so in the background they could listen to the football game between the Chicago Bears and the Cardinals. This was a big game for George Halas and his Bears, as it was the last game of the year before they started the playoffs. They wanted to stay even in the win-loss column with the Green Bay Packers, the only team they had lost to that year. With a record of ten and one, the Bears wanted to make sure they took care of their crosstown rival the same way they did earlier in the year when they played. Coach Halas knew these intercity rivals' games could be dangerous especially if his team is overlooking them and looking ahead to playing the Packers in the playoffs.

Art, who is a Cardinal fan, said he expected a better game than the last time they met.

"Well, I hope so. Didn't the Bears beat them fifty-three to seven last time?" asked Jim.

Art acknowledged the defeat but said that game was at the beginning of the season, and the Cardinals have been improving each week since. "I feel very confident they will make up for that game today."

Jim asked Anna if there were any more potatoes and roast.

Anna replied, "Well, yes, Jim. Would you like both?"

"Please," said Jim.

"Sara," Craig asked, "Art tells me you will be graduating in June. So what are your plans after high school?"

As Sara started to speak, there was an interruption in the football game with a special announcement. Everyone turned to the radio and heard the young announcer from WGN named Ward Quall break in, saying, "We interrupt this broadcast to bring you this announcement from Washington DC. At one twenty-three, Eastern Standard Time today, the Japanese Navy attacked the U.S. Naval base at Pearl Harbor, Hawaii. We will not be returning to the game, but rather, we will stay on the air to bring you up-to-date information as it comes in."

The radio station actually stayed on the air for the next two hundred fifty-seven hours and thirty-five minutes with continuous information on the attack.

Early on, not much was known, and the only information that was available was coming from eyewitnesses who could see the Japanese planes coming into the harbor. There were reports of bombs hitting the water, making large splashes and thick black smoke. Witnesses went on to report wave after wave of Japanese airplanes coming over the rolling green hills of Oahu and into the harbor striking the fleet and the naval base. What was happening or who was winning was unclear. Only those who had a front row seat and were trying to find the words to describe to listeners what was going on knew the sounds and smells of the battle. The reports that were coming in were live, unedited, and at the time unpredictable, which made it difficult for the young announcer to fill the airtime he had because in the radio business, silence was a no-no. It was going to be sometime before the American people would know or see the extent of this attack. However, one thing became certain, and that is the United States no longer had a policy of isolationism. They were about to enter World War II.

No one spoke for several minutes as each sat quietly listening to each word from those reporting the story, trying to make sense of what they were saying and what it meant. They sat with their heads up staring straight ahead, looking past each other as if they were searching to find the future or a hint of the unknown.

Finally, Mary stood, gathering her dishes and said, "I will clear the table." Both Sara and Anna got up and joined her. Craig said nothing as he pushed his chair back from the table, stood, and without speaking, walked into the kitchen. He went to the cabinet above the sink, opened it, and pulled down an unopened bottle of Wild Turkey Whiskey and three glasses. He closed the cabinet and walked back into the living room. He handed Jim and Art a glass, filled them half full, and said, "I think we could use a drink."

Now Craig was not a man who often had a drink in the house, but he kept a bottle in the kitchen for cold evenings, coughs, and special occasions, good or bad. The men said nothing as they brought the glasses to their mouths and drank.

It was the first time Art had ever tasted liquor, so he first took a small sip, getting the taste before finishing the glass with his father and Jim. Craig poured each another as they sat down, still listening to the information coming from the radio. Craig looked to both men seated across from him on the couch and said, "Well, now we know. I think we all knew we would enter the war in Europe, and even though those sneaking Japs couldn't be trusted, I would have never thought they had the guts to do this. Well, now they will learn the power of the United States."

They all sat quietly next to the fire roaring in the fireplace, intently listening to each word from the announcers and eyewitnesses who described the devastation and accounts of this attack. It later became apparent that the attack was successful for the Japanese. They were able to fly bombers, torpedo planes, and fighters from six aircraft carriers positioned outside of Honolulu. They flew right into the harbor without any ships or radar discovering them. Oh, the radar picked up the planes, but the military believed they were American B-17 bombers flying in from the mainland. Therefore, no real notice was given to these activities.

The entire Pacific fleet, which was just waking up, was caught by total surprise, and it took several minutes before anyone understood what was going on. The battleships were all moored in a row and tied to the harbor. For security reasons, all the planes were on the tarmac together, being heavily guarded because the army was concerned about sabotage coming from within the base. The only saving grace was that none of the aircraft carriers was in port at the time of the attack. But just where they were was not known, or they were not saying because they were concerned about the Japanese listening in to gain information.

There were more reports of thick black smoke pouring from the battleships, which had been heavily damaged, but there was no report of the number of casualties suffered with this attack. With each update came more details, and one had to wonder just how our forces could be caught so unprepared and offer so little resistance. When the attack was over, the reports gave a graphic detail of the devastation. Twenty-one American ships were either sunk or damaged. Over two thousand four hundred Americans were killed, and 1,177 of these casualties were sailors and marines who were killed while on board the *USS Arizona* when it sank. Almost two thirds of those who lost their life did so within the first fifteen minutes of the attack. All eight battleships were damaged or destroyed. Another 1,178 Americans were wounded, and 328 aircrafts were destroyed.

There was still much concern that the Japanese would land an invasion force on Hawaii or head east and make a strike against California. Every uniformed active duty soldier, sailor, or marine was ordered to return to his or her base by Monday morning. Those who were on base would stand watch looking over the coastline for any sign of the attacking fleet. However, instead of pushing further east and invading, Admiral Isoroku Yamamoto, the mastermind who planned, initiated, and carried out the most successful military victory in the history of Japan, was turning the entire task force back to Japan to the surprise and objections of everyone, including his own commanders. The terror of the Japanese military would be felt as they, from December 7 to 10, attacked Thailand, Guam, Shanghai, Malaya, Midway, Wake island, and Singapore. They would also drive the British troops from Malaysia. Their quest for total superiority of the Far East and the Pacific was being fulfilled, as one by one the islands in the Pacific fell.

* * * *

The girls had just finished up in the kitchen and were walking into the living room as Mary looked at Craig and said, "I think we need to leave here soon to go cut down our Christmas tree."

Craig was about to object when he realized from the look she had on her face that he should just acknowledge her and go get the hand saw.

"Art," Sara said, "would it be okay if you took me home first? I really would like to be with my family."

"Sure," Art said. "Mom, you go ahead without me. I really don't feel like looking for a Christmas tree tonight."

Mary immediately objected by saying, "Art, you go along and take Sara home. We will wait for you. Tonight, while I have all this family together, we are going as a family to get our tree. I can't do anything about the war and what it will do to our next Christmas, but I can damn sure have this one."

Now Mary only swore when she was either really mad or trying to make her point. So Art didn't say anything. He just nodded and asked if he could borrow the car so he could take Sara home.

Temperatures had dropped to the lower thirties, and snow was falling again as they walked the fields looking for that perfect tree. Mary liked the looks of a Douglas fir but preferred the Northern pine for its long, soft needles and the aroma it provided when it was in the house. She also believed they lasted longer in the house and were less of a risk for a fire. She recalled a Christmas Eve when, as a young girl living in Joplin, Missouri, her father lit the candles on the tree, and it immediately broke out into flames almost burning the house to the ground.

It wasn't long before they all were standing around the perfect tree for Craig to cut down. It was just a little over five feet tall but would be taller once place in the water bucket and brought into the house. The tree looked like it belonged on a Christmas card with thick limbs full of dark green needles and a perfect shape no matter which direction you looked. The needles were long, green, and soft. There was snow sitting on the tips of the branches, giving the appearance that someone had carefully painted each with a brush.

After a brief look over, Mary announced to Craig that this was the one and asked Anna her thoughts. Anna walked around the tree and said, "Well, it would be nice if I could be a little taller."

Everyone laughed because some things just never change no matter how old we get.

Then she said, "I think it is perfect, Mom."

Art looked to his dad and said, "I got it, Dad" as he took the saw and got down on his knees so he could cut it as close to the ground as possible. He pushed and pulled on the saw until the tree fell softly to the ground. With Craig and Jim's help, they carried it to the car where they hoisted the tree to the top and tied it down using the twine Craig had brought from the house.

On the drive home, they watched out the window as the snow continued to fall. You could keep a rhythm with the windshield wipers as they flapped back and forth as if they were keeping time with the snow. The snow was not leaving much moisture on the window, so the wipers squeaked as they rose and fell. Craig said to Mary that he would put the tree outside in a bucket of water this evening, and in the morning, he would trim the lower branches and bring it in the house so she could decorate it. Mary said that would be fine and hoped there would be enough trimmed off so she could make a wreath for the front door.

"I have some large red ribbon that I bought after Christmas last year at O'Hara hardware that should make for a really nice bow on the wreath."

The car grew quiet, and then they heard Mary who was sitting in the back looking out the window gazing into the darkness, as she started to hum her favorite Christmas carol, *Silent Night*." Mary believed it was the one Christmas carol written for those loved ones no longer with them. She believed the words "sleep in heavenly peace" were talking about them. It gave her comfort knowing that, even though they were no longer here in person, they were here in spirit. No one spoke as they listened to the softness of each note from Mary and reflected on today, tomorrow, and what was to come.

When they had arrived home, the men removed the tree from the car and helped Craig get it in a water bucket to sit overnight. It had been a very long day, and it was time for Jim and Anna to say goodbye and head for home. Tomorrow was going to be a difficult day for Jim on his milk route.

As Jim laid his head on the pillow, he thought about all that took place today. He knew their world would be changing, he just wasn't sure when or how. He held Anna in his arms as she laid quietly with her head on his chest. He could feel the softness of her hair as he took in the scent of her perfume and gently stroked her hair when he felt tear drops on his skin.

Anna was also thinking of today. He whispered, "Anna, don't cry. I am not sure what is going to happen, but I will promise you that I will always be here, and we will have our lives together just like we've talked about."

He bent down, kissed her softly, and pulled her closer into his arms taking comfort in the warmth of her body being so close to his. He could feel her heart beating and thought how lucky he was to have her to hold and to love. Jim held Anna in his arms until they both fell asleep.

The next day was hard for everyone, especially after the announcement that President Roosevelt had asked a joint session of Congress to declare war on Japan and also on Germany. In his address, the president said, "Yesterday, December 7, 1941, a date that will live in infamy—the United States of America was suddenly and deliberately attacked by the naval and air force of the Empire of Japan."

The president went on to report the additional attacks that had taken place and then said, "I ask that the Congress declare that since the unprovoked and dastardly attack by Japan on December 7, 1941, a state of war has existed between the United States and the Japanese Empire."

The part of the speech that stuck in Jim's mind was when he said, "No matter how long it may take us to overcome this premeditated invasion, the American people in their righteous might will win through absolute victory. And with the confidence in our armed forces, with the unbending determination of our people, we will gain the inevitable triumph, so help us God."

Jim knew this was a call to the American people to service. So now it was known—no more speculation, no more discussion, no more politics, no more political debates. The United States of America was at war, and it would now be up to his generation to answer the call of service and save mankind.

Chapter 3

A TIME FOR DECISIONS

Jim and Anna hadn't had a lot of opportunities to enjoy the Christmas season. So after supper, they decided to drive downtown to walk the square, do some good old fashion window shopping, and enjoy the decorations that each merchant had on display. Anna especially loved to watch the children and see how excited they were as they stood outside, pressing their noses against the window. They would stand quietly admiring the newest toys on display along with the old standby like electric trains, dolls, Lincoln logs, and toy soldiers. As each child started, you almost could hear their little minds saying, "That one, Santa, I want you to bring me that toy."

Both Jim and Anna were looking for that perfect gift to buy each other on this—their first Christmas as husband and wife. Neither knew exactly what they wanted to buy, and neither had offered any hints or suggestions that may leave a clue as to something they might want. All they had at this point was the limit they had agreed to spend on each other. Maybe a look through windows might offer a hint or maybe a comment that would lead to finding just the right gift.

Ottumwa was a busy community located along the Des Moines River in the southeast part of Iowa. Unlike so many towns found in the

Midwest, Ottumwa's shopping area was not centered around the courthouse but had long streets lined on both sides with merchants and department stores. The tallest building in town was the Hoffman Building, towering over six stories tall. It was best noted for the malts that were freshly made with each order at the drugstore counter. The county courthouse stood on a hill overlooking the town, and a small park was across the street. In the park was a covered bandstand that was used in the spring and summer for outdoor concerts. At the north end of the park was a tall marble monument dedicated to the men of the county who served the union during the Civil War. Their names were listed in alphabetical order along with the regiment they served in and the town they came from. Anna had a great-grandfather named James Henry who marched with Sherman and whose name was listed on the marble stone. She recalled him only slightly from a time when she was very young when they came to visit. She remembered his long white beard, long white hair that touched his shoulders, his strong rough hands, and the gentleness in his voice. She remembers seeing him only twice, the last time on her ninth birthday.

The shops and stores were all lit up and open as it was a very busy night for a Thursday evening. Thursday night was the one night during the week that the town merchants were open until nine. They chose to be open that one evening to accommodate those who worked at John Deere and the local meat packing plant because it was their payday. The merchants stayed open to take advantage of those who would come to the bank and then stay to do any shopping that needed to be done while they were in town.

People could be seen everywhere you looked. Many had their arms filled with bags as they completed their shopping list. Many seemed content doing the same thing Jim and Anna were doing, just walking around and enjoying the sight and sounds of the season. In the park, there were members from the local Methodist church choir who had set up in the covered bandstand and were singing traditional Christmas carols to the crowd that had gathered.

Yes, it was Christmas, and if it weren't for the defense bonds advertising signs and some recruiting posters, one would never know that a war was being waged so far away.

Defense bonds, as they were called in 1941, were series E bonds that could be bought for 75 percent of the face value. They were being supported by merchants, big business, Hollywood actors, and the media all encouraging the people to buy bonds and start a long-term savings plan to help raise the funds needed for this war. Later, in 1942 through 1945, the name would change to "war bonds." These bonds were guaranteed to pay at a minimum of 4 percent twice a year for up to forty years. This wasn't a new idea as it had a history dating all the way back to the Civil War when both the North and the South used the bonds to help supplement the cost of that war. In fact, 62 percent of the funds used by the North came from the sale of this type of bond.

* * * *

After a while, Jim and Anna came to Hoffman's drugstore and Jim asked Anna if she wanted to go inside, sit down, and split a malt. Anna looked inside and said, "Unless you're really set on getting a malt, I'd prefer a cup of hot chocolate and maybe a slice of that carrot cake I saw sitting in the glass container on the counter inside the Coffee Cup Cafe."

Jim agreed that the hot chocolate and carrot cake sounded better than the malt. They crossed the street and entered the café. The bell above the door chimed, announcing their arrival to the merchant. Having a bell above the door was a common practice used by most merchants. Many times they would be in the back or storage area working and not know that someone came into their shop if it wasn't for the jingle sound above the door.

From the kitchen, a voice said, "Welcome, I will be right with you. Have a seat anyplace you want."

"No hurry," said Jim. "We came in to warm up and get a cup or two of hot chocolate and maybe a piece of that carrot cake when you get a chance."

They found a booth, removed their coats, and sat down. Just as the owner was coming over to take their order, the doorbell chimed again. Anna looked over and saw Hazel and her husband Daryl walk in.

"Hazel," Anna called out, "come over here and join us." "What are you kids up to tonight?" asked Hazel.

"Oh, not much. We just came down to look around and get some ideas for Christmas, but mostly, we wanted to just get out of the house for a while. What about you?"

"Well, I guess it is okay to tell you we are looking for baby items." "You're pregnant!" shouted Anna.

"Yes," said Hazel, "but you don't need to tell everyone in the restaurant."

Anna laughed and said, "I'm sorry. I am just so excited for you two. So just when were you planning on telling me?"

"We just came from Doc Rader's office where he confirmed what I already knew. We haven't even told our parents yet, so keep it under your hat."

"So when is the baby due?" asked Anna.

"Well, he says he thinks I am around six weeks, so I guess that would put the due date around the fifteenth of June."

Jim extended his hand to Daryl and offered his congratulations. Daryl reached out and shook hands but didn't look up as he said thanks, not seeming to be as excited as his wife. Hazel asked Daryl if he could slide out as she needed to use the restroom. Anna slid out to go with her.

As the ladies disappeared around the corner, Jim made a comment about ladies always going to the bathroom in pairs and then asked Daryl if he was okay.

"Why do you ask?" said Daryl.

"Well, when Hazel told us about the baby, you seemed a little predisposed."

"Well, I guess I am. You see, this morning I went down to the recruiting office before Hazel had said anything about her being pregnant, and I committed to enlist into the marines."

"Hazel doesn't know?" asked Jim.

"No, I was going to tell her tonight after dinner, but then she mentioned the doctor's appointment and the possibility of a kid, and well, I'm not really sure how to tell her now. Got any suggestions?"

"Gee, Daryl, that's a tough spot," Jim said.

"Well, do me a favor. Don't say anything to Anna until I can figure this out. I am scheduled to go to Des Moines next Thursday to take the physical, and if I pass, I will be a marine and on my way to basic training."

Just as Daryl was reaching into his pocket for a cigarette, he saw the girls coming back to the table. Jim put his pipe into his mouth and lit it as Daryl took a sip of his coffee.

"So, Jim," asked Hazel, "what do you think? Won't Daryl be the greatest dad in the world?"

Jim answered, "That I am sure of, Hazel."

"I hope you guys know we want you both to be our child's godparents."

"Well, of course, I hope you weren't thinking of anyone else," answered Anna.

Hazel and Anna talked, while Daryl sat sipping his coffee and looking out into the evening. When they finished their coffee and coco, the men went up to the counter and paid the tab, while the girls were sharing a hug and saying good evening.

Anna and Jim were heading toward the car when Anna took Jim's arm, snuggled close, and said, "Isn't it great they are having a baby? Hazel is so excited, and I can't wait to help her with the nursery."

Jim looked at Anna and said, "Yes, it is wonderful news, Anna."

But Anna sensed something in Jim's answer and asked, "What is it, Jim?"

"Nothing, I guess it's just with the war going on and not knowing the role we are to play. It just doesn't make for the best time for a baby."

"Are we to put everything on hold because of this war, Jim?" Anna snapped. She realized that there was no reason to have snapped and quickly said, "You're probably right, but God picks the time, and we need to make sure we are there for them and help anyway we can."

Jim placed his arm around Anna, pulled her close, and said, "I know, you're a great friend, and Hazel is lucky to have you by her side. So maybe we should go home and practice making a baby?"

Anna looked at Jim and said, "You're impossible, but maybe."

The next afternoon, Jim called Anna and said he was going to stop by his father's barbershop to get a haircut after he got off work. Jim needed a trim, but what he really had on his mind was how his father avoided serving in World War I and what his thoughts were about this one. He knew his father, like himself, had followed the requirement and had registered for the draft during World War I, but he was not part of the

2.4 million men who were drafted into service during that war. And now once again, the draft was a part of life for the American male.

* * * *

On September 17, 1940, maybe in anticipation of things to come, the Congress of the United States passed and sent to the president for his signature, the Selective Service Training act. This would put into place a peacetime draft where all men from the age of twenty-one to thirty-five were obligated to sign up with their local draft board and become liable for military service. Two days after receipt of the bill, President Roosevelt signed it into law. Now that America was entering World War II, the age would be changed to eighteen to forty-five for military service and up to sixty-five to register.

* * * *

"Good afternoon, Jim, time for a haircut?" Patrick said as Jim entered the barbershop.

"Yes, Dad, if you don't mind, and I also want to talk with you about something that I have on my mind."

"Well, have a seat, son, you're next. I am just finishing up with Doc Shoemaker. Do you know Doctor Shoemaker, Jim?" Patrick asked.

"Yes, I believe we have met before, and I had the pleasure of meeting his daughter Sara when we were over at Craig's house earlier this month."

"Are you related to Art Middleton?" Doc asked.

"Yes, sir, he's my brother-in-law. I married his sister Anna this past July."

"Oh yes, I remember seeing it in the Courier, the local hometown newspaper. The reason I recall is because you guys got married on the Fourth of July, didn't you?"

"Yes, sir," replied Jim, "she also was celebrating her twenty-first birthday. Anna told me later that her father told her right before he walked her down the aisle that she had gained and lost her independence on the same day."

Doc laughed and said, "Well, I guess her father may have been onto something because I guess in some way she did."

"Well, I think you're all done, Doc," Patrick said as he removed the apron around his neck and handed him a hand-held mirror.

"It looks great, Mr. McManis, thank you," he said as he handed him a fifty-cent piece telling him to keep the change. "It was really nice talking with you, Jim. You have a good day, and please tell your lovely bride I said hello."

The doorbell signaled Doc's departure when Patrick turned to Jim and said, "Okay, son, have a seat. I have seen your hair longer than this, so I am wondering what you really have on your mind?"

Jim slid into the seat as his father wrapped the black apron around him and fastened it behind his neck. "Dad, with war coming, I was wondering why you didn't serve in the military during World War I?"

Patrick was taken aback a little from the question as they had never discussed nor had Jim asked about his involvement in the war before today.

"Gee, I guess at the time I did what was required, and I registered with the draft and thought if they needed me they would ask. Why do you ask, Jim?"

"Well, as I said with our involvement now in this war, I believe there is a certain expectation by my friends and especially Anna's family that I serve in some branch of the military. Her father served in the army in the last war and is already talking about serving in the navy along with her brother Art. Our good friend Daryl has enlisted in the marines, and I just believe that I am expected to step up and serve."

"Jim," Patrick said, "are you listening to yourself? You keep mentioning other people's expectations of you. You have to ask yourself, what are your expectations of you? The hell with other people and what they may think. You have to live, or in this case, because it is a war, die based upon this decision, and it should be one you and your wife make together. Ultimately, Jim, it is you that needs to be satisfied with this decision."

"So what was it like being home while other men from the community were overseas?" Jim asked.

"Oh, there will always be those who have something to say no matter what the subject, and they are entitled to that opinion. I suppose the fact that I was still here operating a business instead of being away had a small effect on our business. There were those who decided to either let their hair grow out or went to another barber because I didn't do what they expected and run down to the recruiting station and volunteered. I had an obligation to take care of my family, and as I said, if the government needed my service, they would have drafted me, and I would have proudly served. I find nothing wrong with the service and with those who did serve. Your mother, God rest her soul, kept telling me to go. She would say, 'Patrick, you're as good of a man as any of these men who live in this town, so now you go and show them.' I told her that as long as she believed in me, I didn't really give a damn what others may or may not think. People get themselves in trouble way too often when they pay too much attention to what others think. If I was given the chance to go back and make a decision on this issue again, well, I would do the exact same thing because I am comfortable with the decision I made. You have to be that way on the decision you make, Jim. There, I think you're finished. How did I do?"

Jim looked into the mirror and said, "Just fine, thanks, Dad. As always, you have given me lots to think about."

"So, Jim, have you discussed this with Anna, and do you know which way you want to go?" asked Patrick.

"No, Dad, like you, I am a proud Irish-American, and I will serve without hesitation, and I will fight as well as any man who puts on a uniform. But I believe my greater commitment is to Anna and making sure she will be cared for in my absence. I would like to have some time with her before I am off to the service, but that may not be in my hands. I guess we both have avoided the subject long enough, so maybe it is time we sat down and discussed our future. But first, I think we will enjoy our first Christmas together. The war can wait that long."

Patrick brushed off the loose hair and removed the apron from around Jim's neck as he said, "You're a good man, Jim, and I am confident you will make the right decision for you and your family. Now you owe me two bits for the haircut. The advice was free."

Jim chuckled and thanked his father as he handed him a quarter. As he walked out the door, he turned and said in a very somber voice, "Thanks, Dad."

On his way home, Jim thought of what his father had said and tried to figure out if there was something more that was not said. He knew that sometimes the biggest lesson is not the one you are taught but rather the one you learn by experiencing the lesson. Jim knew, even though he didn't tell his father, that he had made a decision that he would enlist in the military. He understood and respected his father and the decision he had made, but he also believed that one must give back to the society where they live in order to be a part of that society. Commitment, he believed, was the willingness to make a contribution to the community you live in and to its well-being. Jim could not imagine any greater call than the call to defend one's way of life and the freedoms that were being challenged in this war.

He wondered when and how to tell Anna. He knew she would be sad, mad, scared, and proud all in the same moment. He did not want to be like Daryl and Hazel. He and Anna were going to be in this together as a team, and because of that, he knew with their love for each other somehow they could make it through anything the future would throw at them. Jim, however, thought it best to do nothing until after the first of the year. But did that include telling Anna of his plans? That was a question he still did not have an answer for as he pulled into the drive.

As Jim entered the house, he could smell corn bread baking in the oven. He thought to himself cornbread means ham hocks and beans, which was one of his favorite meals. The only drawback to such a meal, of course, was the gas he would have later, but that was of little concern as Jim heard his stomach growl. He approached the stove, lifted the lid from the pot, and was ready to dip the wooden spoon in for a sample when he heard Anna say, "Jim, stay out of that. It won't be ready for another ten to fifteen minutes. You go wash up and have a cup of coffee. There is a fresh pot sitting on the stove. I will be off the phone in just a minute. I am talking to Hazel."

Jim put the lid down and headed over to the sink to wash his hands. As he was washing, he overheard Anna say, "The marines!" Obviously, Daryl had told Hazel of his enlistment plans.

In a few minutes, Anna hung up the phone and went to the stove. She removed the lid and was adding some cornstarch to thicken the soup when she said, "Jim, did you know that Daryl had joined the marines?"

Jim set his cup down on the table and said, "Yes, he told me the other night at the restaurant when you girls went to the bathroom."

"I thought something was up by the way you two were acting. Why didn't you say something to me?" Anna complained.

Jim replied, "Daryl asked me not to until he could figure out a way to tell Hazel. He said he was planning on telling her that evening, but well, the baby news came up, and he knew that wouldn't be the right time. I figured he would have to say something soon because he is going to take his physical on Thursday. So I knew I wouldn't have to keep it from you for long. You're not upset with me, are you?" Jim asked.

"Well, maybe a little. Didn't you think I could keep a secret if you asked? Why would Daryl make such a decision without discussing it first with his wife?"

"I don't know what he was thinking. I know it is a conversation that every married couple will or should have at some point."

"So, Jim, when do you think we will have our discussion?"

Jim was taken aback by the question and thought for a moment. "I guess this is the time I was wondering about."

"So, Anna, what do you think I should do? I know that we have only been married for such a short time, and I want to be here with you, but another part of me says I need to do my duty and join the service."

Anna continued to stir the cornstarch into the soup as she said, "Dad told Mom he thought the three of you would go down to the navy and enlist sometime after the first of the year. Did you guys already talk about the service?" Anna asked.

"We did, kind of. Art asked me with the war breaking out what I was planning on doing, and I said I would probably enlist in the navy. I'm not sure, but I knew that any other answer would only cause more discussion."

Anna said softly, "I guess you have your mind made up?"

Jim went over to the stove, wrapped his arm around Anna's waist, and said. "I would never do anything without discussing it with you first. I not only love you, but you are my partner, and this is something we are going to go through together. I want to have our first Christmas without talking about the war, and I think we have plenty of time after the first of the year to make our plans."

She turned to Jim, and they kissed. Jim held her tight and whispered in her ear, "We are going to be alright, I promise."

Anna said, "I know, but you can't make promises over something you're not sure about or in control of. I know we don't really have a choice, And if you enlist with Dad and Art, at least I will know where the three men in my life are. And maybe then, one of you can keep an eye on the others, so I get you all back safe. Did you speak to your dad today and tell him your decision?"

"No," Jim answered, "we talked about his decision not to join the military in World War I and some of the repercussions it had on him and Mom at the time. He said it is a decision that he does not regret, but I could tell by the things he said, the family was looked upon differently because he stayed home. My father has always had a different look on issues and life events, and what he has to say usually challenges me to think and ask questions so I can see it from a different perspective. He always said if you look within yourself for the answer to the questions that are on your mind, the solution usually becomes very clear. I know it would have been a lot easier for him to just join like everyone else, but he didn't. He has never looked for the easy way, and I wanted to know more about his thoughts on this subject."

Anna turned back to the stove, bent over, and reached into the oven to remove the corn bread. "Jim, put a hot pad on the table and go sit down. We can talk later, but for now, if you're ready, it is time to eat."

Chapter 4

CALLED TO DUTY

....

Jim and Anna had no more discussions about the war and just enjoyed their first Christmas together. They trimmed a small Christmas tree and decorated the house with decorations Anna made from scrap material she had and a few Jim found out in the barn that Doc must have used when he lived in the house. The mantel was decorated with branches cut from the tree, pine cones, and three red candles. They agreed to start their family tradition by opening their presents on Christmas morning and not on Christmas Eve, like Jim's family had done.

Jim's Christmas present to Anna was a white terry cloth robe. He remembered how much she had enjoyed the one that she used at the hotel where they stayed in Chicago when they were on their honeymoon. He found one very similar in the Montgomery Ward's catalog and ordered it in plenty of time, or so he thought. But each day he went to the post office and each day no bathrobe. Finally, the mailman came up to the door and handed Jim the box he was looking for. It was December 24, and the Postal Service had all their carriers out delivering every package that was at the post office to make sure everyone's Christmas present made it to the tree in time. Jim thought to himself how perfect the timing was. He would give Anna her gift one minute after midnight, which would be the first minute of the first hour of their first Christmas.

The final gift he bought for her was a leather-bound photo album that Anna could put their wedding photos in. On the album cover engraved in gold lettering, were their names along with their wedding date. The album had plenty of pages so she could add photos and keep track of their lives and family as it grew.

Anna had a more difficult time finding that one gift but finally decided on two items. The first was a Savage Model 720 automatic shotgun that she knew Jim would like because he really enjoyed being outside and hunting. The second gift had to be something simple because the gun was fifty-two dollars, so she was already over the amount they had agreed to spend on each other. She found and purchased a scrapbook that Jim could take with him while he was away serving in the navy. Neither of them knew at the time that Jim was going to use the scrapbook more than he would ever use the shotgun.

Jim would keep track of his journey, struggles, photos, drawings, newspaper clippings, and letters during every military camp, campaign, and place the war would take him.

It was now March as Jim went to the mailbox and pulled out the mail. Tucked among the other mail was an official letter from the draft board addressed to him. He put the letter in his back pocket and went into the house.

Anna wasn't home from work, as she always worked past five on Thursdays. So he walked out to the front porch, not removing his coat, and sat down on the swing. He looked out the window as he reached for his pipe. He filled the bowl from the leather pouch, lit it, reached into his back pocket, and removed the letter. He examined the envelope. He knew what was inside. Jim glanced at the other mail, but his attention drew back to that letter.

The last couple of days it had snowed, and the trees were heavy from the wet snow. Each limb looked like it was laboring, trying to hold its arms up while the weight of the snow was trying to push them to the ground. You could see some branches had lost the fight as they lay in the yards finished and waiting for spring to be cut up and hauled to the woodpile to become firewood. The setting sun glistened on the snow as if someone had sprinkled glitter.

Jim again picked up the letter and wondered if he should read it now or wait for Anna to come home. He turned the envelope over and ran his finger over it and then eventually under the lip until it was open. He pulled out and opened the one-page trifolded letter and read the lines. As he read each line, his beliefs were confirmed. He was to report to Camp Dodge in Johnston, Iowa, on Tuesday, April 2, 1942, for his physical and induction into the United States Army. He chuckled to himself as he remembered it was April 15 that he, Art and Craig were going to enlist in the navy.

"Well, it looks like I'll be walking in this war instead of riding the high seas," he said out loud. He laid the letter down, relit his pipe, and sat back in the swing. He continued to look out the window being deep in thought as he blew smoke rings over his head and waited for Anna to come home.

It was about ten minutes after five when Jim saw Hazel's car pull into the driveway. He could hear the crunch of the tires as they slowly drove over the frozen snow and the car came to a stop by the back door. He got up from his chair and laid his pipe down as he heard two car doors close. Hazel was coming in.

Jim entered the kitchen the same time as the girls were coming through the door. They stomped their feet to get the snow off their boots and removed their coats and scarves, hanging them on the coat rack. "It sure is cold outside," said Hazel.

"I don't mind the snow, but this bone-biting cold gets really old after Christmas," said Anna. "Jim, do I need to start dinner right away, or can Hazel and I look through the Sears catalog for baby clothes?" Jim asked, "What are we having for dinner tonight?"

"Well, I was thinking we could have liver and onions with fried potatoes or I have some chicken noodle soup I could heat up and have with toasted cheese sandwiches. Do you have a preference?" she asked.

"No," said Jim, "I like both, so whichever is the easiest is good for me." "Okay, then I think we will do the soup," Anna replied.

Jim asked Hazel about Daryl and if he had heard anything about going overseas. "He wrote that it looks like he will be able to get home in June for a while when the baby is born, and everything is well. He says he is becoming a good marine. But it has taken him a while to figure out the gunny sergeant. He says he yells a lot."

Jim laughed and said, "Yeah, I hear they don't have much of a sense of humor. So where is he stationed now?"

"His training group got shipped to join a division at the marine base named Camp Elliott in San Diego. They will be there until September. Then, he says, they are going to the newly built marine base called Camp Pendleton. Daryl thinks the reason they went to the west coast is that his division will be going to the Pacific Theater and not Europe. He says for now there aren't any plans for them to go anywhere, just more training. I am thankful he is still in the good old United States. Jim, are you still thinking about joining the navy?" Hazel asked.

Jim didn't answer, but instead he looked across the table and said, "Anna, do you need me to do anything in the kitchen?"

"No, Jim, I can't think of anything. I will put the soup on the stove to get it warm, and then when Hazel and I are done, I'll toast the sandwiches. Are you hungry?"

"No, I am fine, and if you don't mind, I think I will go into the living room to read the newspaper and leave you girls to look at baby things."

As Jim headed to the living room, Anna turned to Hazel and said, "I have a new ad from Otis furniture store. I left it on the porch. Let me go get it."

Anna went out to the porch to retrieve the catalog but couldn't see, so she turned on the light. As she looked for the ad, she noticed the letter addressed to Jim from the Department of Defense and picked it up. As Anna skimmed the letter, she saw the same words Jim had read just a few minutes earlier: "drafted into the United States Army." She placed the letter back inside the envelope, put it securely inside the pocket of her apron, and headed back to the kitchen. She didn't say a thing but instead handed the ad to Hazel and walked into the living room, took the envelope out of her pocket, and set it down next to Jim. Jim glanced at the table, then to Anna; but before he could speak, she said, "Not now, we can talk after Hazel leaves."

She then turned and walked back into the kitchen. Anna was like a brave soldier never letting on that anything was different and never wearing her feelings on her face.

She said to Hazel, "So do you see anything in the ad you like?"

"I like the bassinet, but I am not sure we can afford it. Maybe if they will extend credit, I might buy it," Hazel replied. "Daryl had written that when he finished his initial training, he would be able to send fifty dollars a month instead of the twenty-one he's sending now. He also said once our child is born, his pay, he thinks, will go to eighty dollars a month. I want to pay my own way, even if I am living with my parents. They really had it hard the last few years, and they can't afford me and this baby, so I will have to see. I can't believe I am going to be a mom in just three months. I am both excited and scared, but I suppose that is normal."

"Well, women have been doing this since the beginning of time, so you are going to be just fine," Anna said, trying to reassure her.

"Well, I had better run and let you two have your supper and get home to help Mom with ours."

Hazel gave Anna a hug and said goodbye to Jim as she put on her coat and headed out the door.

Anna waited until she heard the car leave before she went into the living room. Jim was sitting on the chair looking straight ahead, as if he wasn't even in the same house.

"Jim," Anna said, "when did the letter come?"

"I opened it today when I got home from work. There was no time to tell you with Hazel coming in the house," he replied.

"I know, but what does this letter mean?" she asked. "Can you still join the navy with Dad and Art, or are you in the army?"

"According to the letter, I am to report to Camp Dodge, Iowa, for my physical and induction into the army. If I am qualified, I will be sent to a training camp to start my basic training."

Anna didn't say a word as she reached around, untied her apron, and walked into the bedroom. Jim could hear her sobbing and knew it would be best just to leave her to her feelings for now. Within a few minutes, Anna came out. Her eyes were red, but she gave no indication of being upset. That stubbornness came from the English side in her family heritage; one must keep that stiff upper lip.

She had on her new bathrobe saying, "This was a great present, Jim. I really like my bathrobe. It is soft but mostly snuggly warm. I am going to light the stove to do the sandwiches. Can you set the table?"

"Sure," said Jim, "do you want me to fix a pot of coffee?" "No, I think I will have a glass of milk instead," Anna replied.

"I think I will have a beer tonight. Do we have any in the refrigerator?" Jim asked.

"I think so, and now that you mention it, I think I would prefer to have a beer with you," she replied.

"Anna," Jim said, "you don't drink."

Anna picked up the pot of beans from the stove and as she walked to the table said, "Well, maybe it is time I try."

"Two beers it will be," Jim responded as he opened the refrigerator.

Chapter 5

IN THE ARMY NOW

Jim looked up at the clock in the living room and saw it was half past three. It was Tuesday, April 2, and sitting in the corner of the room was a small overnight bag that Jim had packed for his trip. In the letter Jim received from the draft board, it had explained that he would need to pack enough comfortable clothes and toiletry items to get him through the first few days before uniforms could be issued. Once he was fitted in army green, the items he brought could either be shipped back home or stored away until his training was completed. Jim heard a honk from a car indicating his dad, who had taken the afternoon off, was waiting out front to drive him down to the bus station. Jim picked up his bag, and while standing in the doorway, he turned and took one long look around the house. He looked at each room as if he was trying to capture each moment he had shared with Anna so he could take it with him.

Jim looked over at his dad, while he threw the bag into the backseat.

"Ready, son?" Patrick asked.

"I guess as ready as I am going to be," Jim responded.

Patrick asked about Anna and Jim explained that she was at work. They had said their goodbyes last night, and both agreed this moment would be difficult enough without trying to say goodbye at the bus station. Jim recalled how difficult it was watching Anna walk out the door this morning not knowing when he would see her again or hold her in his arms.

He started to think how unfair it was when his dad interrupted by saying, "Jim, you have to focus on what is now in front of you and trust that you and Anna will be just fine."

"I know, Dad, she is strong, and I know there are plenty of people who will look after her while I am away. So, Dad, have you ever been to Camp Dodge?" Jim asked.

"Once in 1917, when I took a buddy of mine there who went to enlist for the first World War. It seems strange that I would be driving my son to go to the same place for the same purpose."

"Did he come back through Camp Dodge when the war was over?" asked Jim.

There was a pause then Patrick replied, "No, son, he never came home."

Camp Dodge was just outside the capital city of Des Moines. The facility was built in 1907 as a military training base for the Iowa National Guard. Camp Dodge was named after Major General Grenville M. Dodge of Council Bluffs, Iowa's most famous Civil War commander. With the outbreak of World War I in 1917, the facility was expanded to 570 acres and was turned over to the federal government so it could be used as a regional training area for the incoming troops. At the completion of the war, the facility was once again given back to the state of Iowa to maintain and use for their state's militia. Now with the country involvement in World War II, it was expanded to cover six thousand four hundred acres and called back into active federal service for the purpose of inducting and training men who enlisted and who, like Jim, were drafted from Iowa, Nebraska, Minnesota, North and South Dakota to take their turn in fighting this war.

* * * *

As Patrick made the turn into the parking lot of the bus station, Jim looked out the window and saw a line of men with their back to him all checking in for the trip. He stepped out of the car, and as he turned to say goodbye to his father, Patrick had already gotten out of the car and was walking around the front to join him.

He extended his hand and said, "Son, you have already made me proud, and I am confident that you understand your duty. but just remember, your obligation isn't only to this country but to your family and to yourself. I love you, son."

Jim was taken aback by his father's last words and didn't know what to say. Jim couldn't recall the last time his dad had said those words to him. It wasn't that Jim didn't know his father's feelings, but being a proud Irishman, he usually kept what he felt to himself.

Jim grabbed his bag from the car, walked up, and got behind the last man in the line. He listened carefully to the sergeant who was asking each man if they had the documents they would need when they got to Camp Dodge. He went through the list in his head—birth certificate, high school diploma, social security card, and a copy of his marriage license.

He then heard another sergeant yell, "Have your documents out and ready so we can check them. And then get on the bus and take a seat."

Jim stepped up to the table and the sergeant asked, "Last name?" "McManis," Jim responded.

The sergeant found Jim's name on the list, looked over his paperwork, and said, "Okay, you can get on the bus and find a seat."

Jim climbed up the two steps, looked toward the back, and saw all the faces staring back at him.

As he walked to find a seat, he heard a familiar voice say, "Jim McManis, take a seat here."

Jim looked over to the voice and saw the familiar face of Charlie Johansson, a big Swedish kid who played football and was on the high school track and field team with him when they were at Albia High School.

"Charlie, what have you been up to?" asked Jim as he sat down and slid his bag under the seat in front of him.

"Not much. That is why I am on this bus," Charlie replied. "I figured the army could use me, and God knows, I could use the money."

Jim looked out the window to see how many more people were still outside waiting to board and asked, "Oh, so you are volunteering to serve in this man's army?" He then went on to say, "I wanted to join the navy, but I guess I waited too long. I never thought they would get to me this early."

Charlie laughed and said, "Well, maybe we will get stationed together." Just about then, Jim heard the door close and the engine start.

"Okay, men, my name is Sergeant Watson, and for this trip, I will be your contact if you have any questions. I would recommend you sit back, relax, and maybe get some shut-eye. We won't be stopping until we get to Camp Dodge, so you're with me for the next three and half hours."

With that, he started the engine and rolled out of the bus barn turn on to Main Street heading out to old 34 North.

Jim was hungry, so he reached into his paper bag and pulled out the liverwurst sandwich with some sliced red onions that Anna had fixed him. Jim noticed she had packed a green apple and put one small piece of chocolate to tease his sweet tooth. He unscrewed the cup from his thermos and poured himself a cup of coffee. The aroma must have caught Charlie's nose as he turned and looked at Jim and then the coffee. Jim asked if he would like a cup, but Charlie shook his head and replied, "No, thanks. I think I will take the sergeant's suggestion and try to get some sleep."

As Jim ate his sandwich, he looked out the window and saw the last of old man winter still lingering in the fields. Scattered here and there were small piles of snow tucked away and hiding behind anything that would delay them being exposed to the daily sun. It wouldn't be long now before the last of the snowy blanket that had cuddled the earth to keep her warm would give way and provide the moisture to feed the new crops the farmers would be planting. Jim remembered the note Anna had written and reached into his pocket to retrieve it.

He pulled out the small yellow piece of paper that was folded four times, looking like a note he would have gotten from a girlfriend when he was in high school. Jim carefully unfolded each one and read the words Anna had written.

"I am proud of you, Jim, and even prouder to be your wife. I believe our generation was born for this moment to answer this call for service. I am going to be fine, and I will do everything possible here to hasten your return. Now do your duty and get back as soon as you can so we can start our family."

He carefully refolded the note and placed it in his pocket. It would become the first entry into his scrapbook. For now, he thought he would finish his sandwich, join Charlie and the rest of the men on the bus, and get some rest.

Jim had just awakened when the bus made the turn into the camp and came to a stop outside the guard shack. He heard the sliding of the door and saw a young soldier step on to review the papers the sergeant handed him.

As he stepped off, Jim could hear him say, "Go ahead, Sergeant, take them down to the billeting area for their bunk assignments."

As the sergeant closed the door, he barked back at the men to wake up and get their stuff gathered up.

"Listen up! When we stop, I need each one of you to orderly and quickly get off this bus and form a straight line. We will be going inside, and you will be issued bedding and blankets. Once you have signed for them, you will proceed back into the barracks where you will grab a bunk, store your bedding and personal belongings, and then return to the orderly room. We don't have time to make the beds right now, so hurry in and hurry out. Once you are back into the orderly room, you will be broken up into small groups. You will stay with that group throughout this entire process. We have a lot to do and not a lot of time to evaluate and process you for enlistment. So I need you to stay focused and keep the chatter down. Are there any questions? Okay then, fall out!"

Jim had gotten his bedding and was heading back when he heard Charlie saying, "Listen, mister, I ain't looking for any trouble. If you want this bed, you can have it. I will find another one."

The little man answered, "Well, what do we have here? It looks like a big dumb farmer boy who wants to join the army but is afraid of a fight."

Just as Jim was entering the room, he saw Charlie hit the man who was speaking. Charlie hit him so hard that he not only fell over one bunk but slid under the bunk next to it. The commotion brought the sergeant in yelling.

"What in the Sam hell is going on in here?"

Jim was reaching down to pick up the man and said, "Nothing, Sergeant, he just tripped over the bunk. I guess he didn't see it."

Everyone laughed as the sergeant grunted and yelled. "Okay, men, let's get moving."

Jim reached out his hand to stop the man from going after Charlie and said, "My name is Jim, and that is Charlie. He is a gentle soul unless you get him riled up. But I guess you know that now."

The other guy looked at him as he rubbed his chin and said, "Is he a man or a damn mule? My god, I have felt better after being kicked by one. My name is Henry."

Charlie came over and extended his hand and said, "Sorry mister, I really didn't want to hit you but you made me mad."

Henry said nothing, but just shook his hand and they all walked out together and joined the line. They started to count off . . . one, two, three repeating again after reaching three.

Once they were done, the sergeant said, "Okay, the ones will come with me; the twos will stay here; and the threes will get back on the bus and go with Sergeant Watson."

Jim and his new friend Henry were both ones, so they followed the sergeant across the street into another building. Once inside, Jim glanced around the large room. In front of him were several tables with chairs and several soldiers just mingling around looking at them. They were told to find a seat at any of the tables in front of them and sit down. They were to leave one seat open between them and the next guy so there would be no temptation to look at the other fellow's answer sheet. Soon, an army officer stepped up to a podium, introduced himself, and started giving a brief explanation as to what they were about to do.

He said, "The test you are about to take will be measuring different skills you have, and the results will allow us to match those skills to specific jobs that you could be doing in the army or the marine corps. Does anyone have any questions before we begin?"

In the back of the room, a man spoke up and asked, "So if I understand you correctly, this test will match us to a job we can do in either the army or the marines but not the navy?"

"That is correct," said the Lieutenant. "As I said, they have their own test, and you are here to be inducted into one of the branches which you are now testing for. Would there be any other questions before we get started? You will be given one hour and thirty minutes to complete this exam. Please do your best, and when you are done, you are to lay your pencil down, leave your booklet on the table upside down, and go outside. Stay in the front of this building, and someone will come get you when the time is up.

* * * *

The test they were about to take replaced the Army Alpha and the Army Beta test that was used during World War I. It was similar in the type of questioning, but it was now called the Army General Classification Test or AGCT. Later in the years to come, additional testing would be introduced that would test specific aptitude and skills to include language.

Jim opened the booklet, read each question carefully, and then marked his answer on another sheet of paper by filling in the circle that corresponded to that question. Jim wasn't finding the questions too difficult as they covered topics from mechanical, mathematical, logic, and even some first aid. As he read the question, he occasionally thought, *How will this question tell them anything about a job in the service?* But he remembered the lieutenant saying they only had an hour and half, so he had better just answer and let the military figure out the reasoning for the question.

Once the testing was over, the men were taken back to the barracks and told they were to get a good night's sleep, as tomorrow they would start their day at 0530 hours. Charlie, Jim, and Henry sat briefly talking about home and the military test they had just completed. Henry was from a small town outside Minneapolis called Inver Grove Heights. He worked in a small family owned shoe store, and like Jim, he received a draft notice. After a few minutes, the sergeant came in and yelled "lights out," and the men turned in.

Five thirty in the morning came soon enough as the lights went on, and there was a man standing in the room barking instructions for them to get up, get dressed, and be outside of the orderly room in thirty minutes. Jim got out of his bunk and realized the barracks had the same cold wooden floors he had in the house he and Anna lived in, which didn't help the urge he had to pee. The bathroom had one wall in the middle, and there were eight sinks and mirrors on each side. On the outside wall were urinals, and against the back wall were fourteen toilets all in a row. Jim laughed and thought to himself that this arrangement would make it easy to pass the toilet paper. He quickly shaved, brushed his teeth, and combed his hair. As he headed outside, he remembered his coat as the sun hadn't been told to rise yet, and he knew there would be a chill in the air. The men mingled and smoked as they waited for their instructions as to how they were going to begin their day. Just as Jim was lighting his pipe, a bus pulled up, and the men were instructed to board so they could be taken to breakfast. When the bus stopped, they all filled into a very large and noisy room where men from all over the Midwest were eating. There were several rows of long tables all leading up to a serving area where there were men in white shirts and hats serving up the food. The air was filled with the smell of sausage, flapjacks, eggs, biscuits, gravy, and fresh coffee.

Jim gathered in all the smells and said to Charlie, "Well, it looks like the army knows how to eat."

Charlie wasn't paying too much attention as his only thought was to get as much of this food as he could before they were told to get back on the bus. Both men gathered a large silver tray, placed the silverware in their pockets, and were starting through the line when Henry came up and said they seemed to have everything but fresh fruit. Charlie was about to take a seat at the table when he spotted a table with baskets of fruit. So instead of sitting, he headed in that direction. He pocketed an apple and a banana.

When he got back to the table, he told Jim this would give him something for a snack later.

The men were allowed enough time to enjoy a very hearty breakfast and to step outside for a smoke before they were once again divided up in their groups and shuttled off to continue their testing. Jim and Henry were taken to the infirmary for their physical exam. As they approached the door, a young private handed them some papers, a pencil and told them to go over to the table, complete the medical questions, and then follow the yellow line on the floor through each station until they saw the doctor.

As Jim opened the folder, it appeared the questions were the same he had answered earlier at the recruiting office. They were about childhood illnesses like mumps, asthma, and then questions about his parents' medical history. When he completed the forms, he left them on the table as they were instructed and starting following the yellow line. When he got to the eye station, a lady asked him if he wore glasses or was ever told he needed to have glasses. Jim answered no as she handed him a small paddle instructing him to place it over his left eye and read line 5. "O P V S Q T R."

"Okay, now do the same with your right eye," she said.

Jim repeated the procedure, and when he was finished, she took the paddle and told him to follow the line on the floor and go see the dentist. As Jim walked over, he knew his teeth weren't the greatest because of the times and the fact that there wasn't a lot of money to be spent on a dentist when he was growing up. He said to himself unless they wanted him to bite the enemy, he wasn't sure what the issue would be. He took a seat in the chair, and the dentist immediately started looking into his mouth and calling numbers out to his nurse. He wasn't sure what the numbers indicated, but he understood the doctor when he would say "missing." As a kid, if you got a toothache, Dad pulled it out, and you moved on.

When the doctor was done, he said to his nurse, "Put a note in his file that he is a candidate for dentures."

"Yes, sir!" she answered as she took the towel from Jim's neck and told him to follow the line to the doctor.

Jim followed the lines that led him to a closed door, and after knocking, he turned the knob and walked in. Once inside, he was told to strip off all of his clothing down to his shorts and get in line. He felt like a cow going to slaughter as each man in front of him stepped forward. They probed first inside his mouth and then ears, and finally the doctor listened to his chest. He joined six other men who were standing in line with their back to the doctor.

He heard the doctor say, "Okay, boys, drop the shorts, bend over, and spread your cheeks."

Just as Jim was following the instructions, he heard a commotion and then laughter. Jim looked down the row and saw some poor bastard who apparently didn't realize the doctor meant his butt cheeks and was bent over spreading his mouth.

"Are you an idiot or a fool?" The doctor screamed as he turned him around and bent him over. Once each man was examined, they were told to pull their shorts up and follow the line to the next room.

Once again, Jim opened the door and walked into a large room where he saw four rows of men each walking through their lines receiving shots. Five shots total, two in each arm and one in the butt.

After Jim's last inoculation, he turned back to the nurse and said, "That last one really hurt. What was it?"

She answered, "It was gamma globule, which is a very thick syrup given to help build a soldier's immune system and help prevent you from catching disease once you're overseas. If you think it hurts now, just wait."

Jim went over, got dressed, and walked outside where he saw many men limping and rubbing their arms. He finally saw Henry come out and asked, "How did you do?"

"Oh, it was okay, but that damn last shot hurt like hell going in, and I can hardly walk now," Henry answered.

Jim explained what he was told from the nurse and said he figured they would be able to walk it off soon. A truck pulled up, and two men jumped out walking around to the tailgate and yelling for the men to line up for lunch. Now Jim wasn't very hungry, so he stayed and lit his pipe.

As he blew out a smoke ring, he heard a man from behind him say, "Well, I know you're not deaf or you wouldn't be out here. So that means you are either not hungry or stupid."

Jim quickly turned around to see the largest man he had ever seen speaking to him. This man was at least six feet and seven inches tall and had to weigh at least two hundred and sixty pounds if he weighed an ounce. The muscles in his upper chest pushed and strained the buttons on his shirt, and Jim could see the sleeves in his shirt were in the same shape. His uniform was as sharp and pressed as it could be. The only wrinkles were the ones that were starched and pressed in. This man's eyes were black and told a story you didn't really want to hear. And the way he curled his mouth as he spoke reminded Jim of a bulldog waiting for lunch.

"Son, you're not at home anymore, and here when you are told to do something, you just do it. Do you understand me?" the sergeant yelled.

"Yes, sir," Jim immediately answered as he quickly walked to the truck. Henry looked at Jim and said, "Who shit in his lunch pail?"

Jim answered, "I'm not sure, but I'm not thinking I will ask him today." They were given metal trays as one of the men placed a slice of bread on the tray, while the other served some sort of meat gravy over it along with a cup of black beans.

"Coffee is by the front bumper if you want something to drink," said the corporal.

Henry looked at his plate and said, "My god, the quality of the food sure has gone downhill since breakfast."

Jim snickered, "I guess now that they know we passed the physical, they don't have to impress us anymore."

After lunch, they walked the quarter mile over to the orderly room where they would sit and wait their turn to see the counselor. Here they were to discover what the army had in store for them and where and when they would be going to begin their training. There was a lot of speculation, but mostly, the men just took the opportunity to sit quietly and catch a few minutes of sleep.

Finally, Jim heard a man yell. "McManis!" Jim rose and followed the man into a room where he was instructed to take a seat behind a table.

"McManis," a young second lieutenant said as he turned around to pull out a seat. "You're going into coastal field artillery where we will take advantage of your math skills. You will be leaving on Wednesday for Fort Worden located in Port Townsend, Washington. There, you will spend the first twelve weeks learning how to become a soldier and then another fifteen weeks learning your assignment in the artillery. Do you have any questions?"

Jim looked at the map behind the lieutenant and asked if he was allowed to contact his wife and share this information with her? The lieutenant said he would, but for security purposes, he could not make contact until after his arrival at Fort Worden. Once there, and after he had been assigned to barracks, received uniforms, and got settled, he would be given time to pack his civilian things, send them home or place them in storage, and then and only then could he write a letter to his family.

Jim asked if there was anything else, and the lieutenant said no as he extended his hand and wished him good luck. Jim slid his chair back and went to a small room where there was a podium. To the right was an American flag, and on the left was the flag of the United States Army. There were seventeen men seated and just waiting—for what, they were not sure. But they didn't have to wonder long as a major walked into the room, and the men were summoned to their feet.

The major introduced himself and told them he would be extending the oath of enlistment. They remained standing as they raised their right hand and recited the following: "I, stating their full given name, do solemnly swear (or affirm) that I will support and defend the Constitution of the United States against all enemies, foreign and domestic; that I will bear true faith and allegiance to the same; and that I will obey the orders of the President of the United States and the orders of the officers appointed over me, according to regulations and the Uniform Code of Military Justice. So help me, God."

Once completed, the major came to shake each man's hand and render a hand salute. He then walked out of the room. The sergeant came in and told them they were dismissed. They could go back to the barracks, and the rest of the day was theirs. They could not leave the base, and they could not make any contact with anyone outside of the base.

As Jim was walking back to the barracks, his thoughts turned to Anna; and even though he would be leaving tomorrow, it was a strain not to call her and share his information. He said to himself, *Well, you're in the army now, so I had better get used to that and do everything their way, or this could be a long and very difficult time.*

About then, Henry and Charlie came up announcing they too had received their orders. Henry was going to medical training at Fort Jackson, and Charlie was going to Fort Gordon to train in the infantry. Charlie started singing "We're in the army now, we got our head in the cloud, you will never get rich digging a ditch, we're in the army now."

Jim chuckled and said, "Yes, Charlie, we certainly are."

Chapter 6

SETTLING IN

Anna looked up at the clock as she removed her headset and hung it up next to her panel. It was five in the afternoon, and the end of her shift had finally come in what was a very long day. As she exited the phone company, she ran across the street to catch the trolley that was just pulling up to the curb. Anna didn't mind riding the trolley, but most of the time, Jim would be there to pick her up. Now with Jim being gone, she realized that the luxury of choosing was no longer an option, and that this ride would become a part of her daily routine.

Anna looked up to see they were approaching her stop, so she reached up, and she pulled the cord notifying the driver that she would be getting off. Anna said good evening to the driver as she stepped off the trolley and made the one block walk to her house. As she hung up her coat and scarf, her first notion was to call out to Jim, letting him know she was home, but she realized he wasn't there. She put her purse down and walked out to the front porch where she caught the aroma of Jim's pipe. Anna walked over to the chair where Jim would sit after dinner and enjoy his pipe. As she looked out across the neighborhood she could see the children running and laughing as they played in their yards. Their life appeared to be so simple and normal, but she knew her life, like so many other families', was changing. As Anna sat there, she felt a sudden chill, not from the coldness of the evening but from the realization that for the first time in her life, she was alone and just how much she missed Jim.

The longer she sat there, the more her thoughts were of him. What was he doing? When would she see him again, and was he missing her as much as she was him? Hazel had told Anna it could be some time before she would hear from him, but she had to trust that no news was good news. Anna rose from the chair and headed back into the house. She wanted to change her clothes and put on her bathrobe before she started supper. She didn't know what she wanted, but she knew cooking for one and sitting at the table alone wasn't going to be a lot of fun.

Anna was coming out of the bedroom, and as she was tying her sash, she heard the phone ring. She hurried to the phone, thinking it was Jim, and said hello. It wasn't Jim; it was Hazel who heard the disappointment in Ann's voice.

"Sorry, Hon, it's just me," Hazel said. "I take it you haven't heard from Jim yet?"

"No, but he will call when he can," replied Anna. "So what's up?"
"Well, I was hoping you hadn't started your supper yet, and we could go downtown to grab a bite and then pick up the cradle I had on hold from Montgomery Ward's."

Anna paused for a minute as she was tired and really didn't want to go anywhere. But she also heard the excitement in Hazel's voice and answered, "I will get dressed, and you come pick me up."

"Great, I will honk when I get there," Hazel answered.

The girls decided to stop in at Micki's Cafe, a little diner that sat on the shoreline of the Des Moines River. It wasn't a very big restaurant with only ten tables, but the view and the quaintness of the décor made it a special place to go. This is where Jim and Anna had their first real date, and it was along that same river bank that Jim had asked Anna to marry him. The girls went to a table in the Corner where they could talk and look out over the river. The heavy winter snow had melted and filled the river, so the banks were straining to keep all the water in line and moving down toward the old Mississippi. There was some concern and a great deal of talk that too much early spring rains could push that river over the banks, and there could be flooding like the one they had experienced in thirty-eight. That year, the water came out over the banks in full force pushing its way into town and neighborhoods, damaging anything and everything that stood in its way. One of those homes was her parents.

Because the girls worked different shifts now, they hadn't had a chance to talk for the last few days. Anna broke the silence. "Hazel, have you heard anything from Daryl?"

Hazel replied that she received a letter yesterday from him, and there wasn't any change in what he had already told her. He expected to be sent over to the Pacific, but no one was saying where or when. So the plan for now was that Daryl would get some leave and be home in time for the baby's birth.

Hazel looked at Anna and asked how she was doing with this being the first night away from Jim, which was the real reason for Hazel's call, knowing Anna might enjoy some company.

"Oh, I am fine. I think about him and wonder what he is doing and where he will be going and hoping the phone will ring, but I know you said be patient."

Hazel said, "It gets a little easier each day. You just need to depend on the family and friends to keep your sanity during these times we are now in."

Anna agreed as she picked up the menu. The special for this evening was beef and noodles over mashed potatoes, cooked carrots, and a small garden salad with a dinner roll. Both girls ordered the special and continued their conversation about everything that was going on.

After dinner, the waitress dropped off the bill, and Hazel went to pick up the tab, but Anna would have none of it, stating that Hazel needed to save her money. They asked for a refill of their coffee when Hazel opened her purse and took out a cigarette and lit it.

Anna paused a second and then said, "Hazel, when did you start smoking?"

"Shortly after Daryl left. I find it relaxes me and gives me a chance to unwind a little," she replied. "Would you like one?"

"No, thanks," replied Anna. "I think I will stick to just my coffee." They finished their coffee, paid the bill, and headed to the parking lot to make the short drive to downtown before the stores closed.

The girls entered Ward's, and Hazel went to the counter where she found a sales person standing and asked if she could retrieve an order that was being held for her on layaway. The salesman asked her name and went to the back of the store. Hazel told Anna that her mother thought the money spent on a cradle was a waste because the baby would soon grow out of it, and then she would need a crib.

Anna asked, "Where did your mother propose the baby would sleep in the meantime?"

Hazel answered, "I guess like I did when I was first born . . . in the bottom drawer of the dresser."

Both girls laughed, and Anna said, "Well, I guess if the baby was making too much noise, you could just close the drawer."

The salesman returned pushing a cart that had the cradle on it. He took the remaining payment and then asked if she would need any assistance getting it in her car. Hazel thanked him and said she thought they could handle it from there.

Once home, the girls got the cradle out of the car and into Hazel's parents' house.

Mr. Roberts, John came over, gave Anna a hug, and said, "Well, what do we have here?"

Hazel replied, "It's the cradle, Dad. I had it on layaway, and we went down tonight and made the final payment so we could bring it home. Can you help us put it together?"

John reached into his pocket to retrieve his pocket knife so he could open the box. He glanced at the instructions and said, "Well, this shouldn't take us too long."

As he was putting the pieces together, Hazel's mother, Martha, came in and, seeing the girls, said hello. She looked over to John and made a comment that he should wait before he put the cradle together because being in a hurry can be bad luck.

"Oh, Martha," John said, "you and your superstitions. I don't think a few screws will change the course of the birth of our grandchild."

About that time, the cuckoo clock crowded out eight times. Anna said that it was getting late and that she still had a few things she needed to do before she turned in for the night. Anna gave both Martha and John a hug goodbye as she and Hazel went to the car.

* * * *

It was ten in the evening as the lights were going out in the barracks. In the background, you could hear the faint sound of "Taps" being played reminding all who could hear that this day was done. Jim lay in his bunk looking up at the ceiling. His thoughts were of Anna and the train trip he would be taking tomorrow. He wanted to get to his new assignment so he could let Anna know where he was and that he was okay, knowing that she would be worried. He also had mixed emotions about leaving Iowa, remembering what his father had said about his best friend who never came home.

Over in the next bunk, Jim heard Henry calling his name. "Jim, can you imagine I am going to be a medic? What the hell did they see in the test that I don't know? I get sick when I see blood, and let's not even go there if you're throwing up."

Jim asked, "Did you tell them that when they gave you this assignment?"

"Hell, yes, and you want to know what they said! They said you will eventually stop throwing up and be a great doc."

Jim only could laugh and said, "Well, the army is supposed to know about this stuff, so who knows, you might be great and find a new career. What did you do before this?"

Henry laughed and said, "I was a shoe salesman." Eventually, the men stopped talking, allowing their minds to clear as they drifted off to sleep.

The morning came fast enough when the sergeant entered the room, threw on all the lights, and started barking orders for the men to rise and get the day started. Jim looked out the window, saw it was still pitch black, and said to himself, before we start a new day, maybe we should at least let the last one finish.

Charlie was already in the shower, and Henry was on the throne as each man in the barracks went about their business preparing to depart on their own journey. There wasn't much time for talking as the excitement of the day trumped any need to visit.

There were green canvas-covered trucks lined up in front of the barracks, and the men were told to grab their personal belongings and get into one.

Sergeant Watson yelled, "It doesn't matter which truck you men chose. They all are heading for the same place."

Once they arrived at the Des Moines train station, the men were separated into three groups. Some, like Henry, were going east; some, like Jim, west; and most, like Charlie, to combat infantry training at Fort Leonard Wood, Missouri. There wasn't much time for goodbyes, but each man found the time to shake a few hands, wish each luck, and hope they got home safely. For Jim, he was directed to the rear of the train where there were three Pullman cars attached for military personnel.

Now Pullman cars were named after George Pullman who, after a long miserable night and long train rides from Buffalo to Westfield, New York, awoke with an aching back and an idea. The discomfort of sleeping upright in his seat inspired him to design a more comfortable passenger rail car with sleeper berths for passengers. Pullman's sleeping cars were designed to allow a sleeping berth for all passengers riding in the car. During the day, the berth would be folded up and hidden away. At nighttime, the bunks would be lowered over the two seats below it. There were curtains for privacy and separate washrooms at each end of the car for the men. These standard models, while certainly not luxurious, were a huge improvement over sleeping in your seat. Mr. Pullman also went on to design the dining car, which meant trains could travel longer distances because they did not have to stop to allow their passengers the time to get off, eat, and then reboard to resume their trip.

During the second World War, the U.S. Defense Department would rent and attach thousands of cars to trains all over the United States to transport military men and women from every branch of the service to their stateside assignments. These cars became the mainstay for train travel, not just during the war years but for the next two decades. That, of course, ended once air transportation costs started to become more affordable.

* * * *

Once Jim boarded, he was surprised to see there were already a few men in the car. Apparently, this train had originated from Chicago and, like himself, was heading to Port Townsend. The corporal checked off Jim's name and told him to sit any place that was open. Jim didn't know a soul, and to his surprise, he and another young man he had not met yet were the only two men coming from Camp Dodge. He found an open seat and stowed his suitcase under it. As he sat down, a guy came up from behind him and said, "So how many years did the judge give you?"

Jim turned toward the voice and replied, "What? I didn't get sent here by the courts. I am here because of the draft board!"

The man responded, "That lousy judge and the double-crossing attorney of mine gave me the choice of joining the army or serving ten years in the state pen. I was framed, I am telling you, and I think my father may have been behind the whole dirty deal."

He stuck out his hand and introduced himself. "Ray Mansini, but my friends call me Shorty."

Now Ray stood about five seven and weighed about one hundred and sixty to seventy pounds. His hair was jet black and slicked straight back. His eyes were a dark brown, and his skin was an olive tone. Under his left eye, he had a scar that ran about three inches from his eye to his nose. The suit he had on indicated he came from money, as the inside was lined with silk, and it probably cost, well, over three hundred dollars.

He had a cigar in his left hand, and when he saw Jim glance down at it, he announced, "Same brand Big Al (Capone) liked to smoke."

Ray went on, in a very boisterous voice, that he was from Chicago and then asked Jim, "Where are you from, boy?"

"Ottumwa, Iowa," Jim replied as he sat back down in his seat. "So, Ray, what did you do in Chicago?"

Ray took a moment to look into Jim's face and said, "Really, you have never heard of the Mansini family from Chicago?"

Jim, who was somewhat taken aback by the question, said, "Sorry, no, I haven't."

Ray laughed out loud and said, "That's okay. I doubt you get much news out on the farm. My family runs a very large business on the south side, and I am a loan officer for them. Do you know who Arky Vaughan is?"

Jim answered, "Yes, why do you ask?"

"Because when I first saw you, I thought you were him." answered Ray.

Now Joseph Floyd Vaughan was a baseball player who played for the Pittsburg Pirates and the Brooklyn Dodgers. He played shortstop or third base for fourteen seasons between 1932 and 1948. And he would eventually be elected into the baseball hall of fame in 1985.

* * * *

Ray went on to say, "You could be his twin, so I think I am going to call you Arky, unless you have a problem with that."

Jim smiled and said, "No problem for me. I guess everyone should have a nickname, and that one is better than some I've heard."

There was only one man on the train who was in uniform, and that was the corporal who took Jim's name when he first got on. He told Jim everyone on this train and everyone they would be picking up would be going to Fort Worden for training. Jim sat in his seat enjoying the scenery when the corporal came by and handed him an army basic military training manual.

"Men, here are some reading materials that you might want to find some time to read while you're on this train for the next two days. You will find it details many of the things you will be expected to do as soldiers. Pay attention to the terminology so you understand the commands that are given and that you will be expected to follow."

He went on to tell them that they were to stay in this car or the dining car, as it was important that they maintain the integrity of the group and that they were not to disembark the train at any time unless told to do so.

Jim opened the book and started to glance through the pages, noticing it covered areas from close-order drill, commands, weapons, first aid, and dress. Ray looked at the manual, laid it down in his seat, and lit his cigar, saying, "Some things just have to wait."

At each stop, a man or two would get on the train, and the number in the car, when they stopped in Kalispell Montana, had grown from three when Jim got on to ten. At Kalispell, the men were allowed to get off the train, use the restroom in the station, smoke, and stretch their legs while a maintenance crew worked on the engine. They were to be ready to reboard upon the command, so they shouldn't drift too far.

Jim was enjoying his pipe when the corporal came up to him and said this delay was probably going to last four hours or so and that he might want to grab a cup of coffee or a sandwich inside the station.

Jim noticed the last name on the corporal's blouse and said, "Thanks, Corporal Mitchell, can you tell me how much further we have to go before arriving in Port Townsend?"

The corporal reached inside his shirt pocket, pulled out a pack of Pall Mall, lit one, and answered that once the train was rolling again, they had one more stop to make to pick up additional recruits and then should be arriving in Seattle in about nine hours. From there, they would board a bus for a ride to Port Townsend and then on to Fort Worden which would take another two and half to three hours.

Corporal Mitchell then snickered and said, "You are familiar with the history of the trains and their ability to maintain their schedule? So who knows for sure?"

Jim thought back to the train he would hear each morning in Ottumwa and how it was always late, so he acknowledged his familiarity with trains and their schedule.

The men were asleep when they heard the corporal coming through the car telling them to get up, put their bunks away, and get their belongings together as they were coming into Seattle. Jim glanced at his watch and saw it was four-thirty in the morning and wondered if the army ever slept in. The corporal was right. What should have taken nine hours took a little over eleven, but Jim was thankful they were allowed to sleep until four because had the train been on time it would be one thirty, and Ray would have had a real problem with that.

As Jim stepped off the train, he felt the coldness in the air and realized Washington was a lot colder than Iowa for being early April. He slipped on his coat and started his walk over to the bus when he heard a big loud voice yell out, "Fall in."

Jim stopped, remembering that command from the manual, quickly turned around, and ran over to a line where the men were assembling.

Three men in uniform stood in front of them wearing their olive drab wool uniforms that were neatly pressed with leggings that were tied neatly around their highly spit-shined tanned boot. They had on wool garrison caps, with the insignia of the Fourteenth Coastal Artillery Regiment, to guard against the cold olive drab cotton field jackets. According to the stripes they were wearing on their sleeves, each of the men were sergeants. As Jim was trying to remember their ranks and who was in charge, one of them stepped up and introduced himself as First Sergeant Fisher.

He said, "Men, in the army, the first name can be found on the sleeve or collar, and the last name is printed over the right shirt pocket. So you can call me First Sergeant Fisher. To my right is Tec Sergeant Henderson, and to his right is Sergeant Lee, and you have already met Corporal Mitchell. For the next several weeks, we are going to be in charge of your training. We will be your father, mother, brother, teacher, and preacher because we are going to spend so much time together you will think we are related. When we are finished with your training, you will either be soldiers or in the stockade. Are there any questions?" He paused briefly and said, "If not, I need you to form a single line and get on that bus. The only sound I want to hear is your tired ass feet dragging against the ground. Now move!"

The sun peeked its way over the harbor and allowed Jim to see the Pacific Ocean for the first time. He nudged Ray who grunted that he was more interested in catching some zees than sightseeing. Jim stared out the window and was amazed just how large the ocean was. He knew it was big, but photos really cannot capture the magnitude and magnificent of this body of water. Jim was a little disappointed that it didn't appear to be as blue as he had imagined but rather a shade of blue green. He watched the waves as they lazily came rolling in with the tide. Each wave smashed against the stones bathing them entirely then gently retreating back to where they came. He looked to the horizon to see if he could see any ships or fishing boats going out for the day, but the cloud cover and fog was still too heavy to see much. He strained to continue to watch the water, but as the bus turned, the ocean fell out of sight, and it wasn't long before Jim caught sight of the main gate of the fort. Jim, realizing they would be arriving soon, continued to nudge Ray until he woke.

"Now what the hell is going on?" asked Ray.

"I thought it would be best if you woke up. We are approaching the main gate, and I would imagine someone with a bad attitude will be jumping on this bus very soon and barking out commands," answered Jim.

Ray looked out the window and asked Jim where the ocean was. Jim laughed and said, "We passed it a while back. I tried to wake you, but you wanted to sleep, so I guess you will have to see it some other time."

Just as Jim had predicted, a man in uniform came on the bus and started yelling for everyone to get out and fall in at the grass area on his right. Without hesitation, Jim bolted from the bus and stood motionless awaiting the next command. Ray, on the other hand, came strolling off the bus, reached into his pocket, and pulled out a cigar. He was just about to light it when the sergeant came up and got right in his face. Ray stood there not making a sound or moving, the cigar hanging out the left side of his mouth.

"Just what in the Sam hell do you think you are doing?" the sergeant asked in a calm but loud voice. "I do not believe I heard anyone say smoke break?"

He grabbed the cigar out of Ray's mouth and threw it on the ground, crunching it under his boot. "Now unless you want to sweep this area up with a toothbrush, I would suggest you move your ass over to that formation and join the other men, and I mean RIGHT NOW!"

Ray started to protest but thought better of it as he glanced down at the cigar, mumbled something, and joined the other men in the formation.

"Welcome to Fort Wordon, home to the 14th Coastal Artillery Regiment and the 248th Regiment of the Washington National Guard. We share this space with the navy and the 2nd Amphibious Engineers. You already know my name, and for now, I don't give a crap about yours or where you are from." The first sergeant went on to say, "Today, you start your journey to become American soldiers, and let's make no mistake. You will become soldiers. Some of you volunteered, and for that, this nation is grateful. But most of you did not. Your country is even more in debt to you because it will be your sacrifice that will eventually lead us to total and complete victory and the end of this war. We didn't ask for this fight, but we are in it, and our success is based upon your acceptance of your role in this war and this army. Today, you will be issued the basic uniforms that you will need while training, along with other basic necessities such as shaving equipment, shoe polish, etc. You will get your bedding along with your assigned quarters, and then you will have time to write letters home. I highly encourage you to write because I will not guarantee that you will get that much time again. There are no phones available for calls, so don't ask. With your free time, you might want to tour the base and learn something about its history, but you may not leave this base for any reason. Any attempt by any one of you for any reason will result in the harshest of punishment. Are there any questions before I turn you over to Corporal Mitchell?"

From the back of the formation, they heard the command, "Attention!" And even though they weren't sure what that exactly meant, they all stood tall and did not move. "Fall out."

* * * *

Fort Worden is located in Port Townsend, Washington, along Admiralty Inlet. The fort sits on 433 acres and was built to be used as a United States Army installation for the protection of Puget Sound. Fort Worden was named after Navy Admiral John Lorimer Worden who was the commander of the *USS Monitor* during the American Civil War. The Admiralty Inlet was considered so strategically important to the defense of Puget Sound in the 1890s that three forts—Fort Worden, Fort Flagler, and Fort Casey—were built at the entrance, and huge guns were installed to create a "Triangle of Fire" that could theoretically ward off any invasion attempt by sea. Fort Worden sits at the extreme northeastern tip of the Olympic Peninsula on a bluff near Port Townsend. In the long history of the fort, it never once fired a hostile shot, and the guns were removed and used during World War I in Europe. Subsequently, Fort Worden was used for training military personnel and for other defense purposes from that time forward.

* * * *

Once settled in, Jim lay down on his freshly made bunk and started a letter off to Anna. He wanted to let her know where he was, where she could write, and what he had been up to these past few days leading up to his first week. He glanced around the room and saw, in the corner of the barracks, men making their bunks, introducing themselves, and trying to get settled. These barracks were similar to the one Jim had stayed in at Camp Dodge. On each side of the room were twenty-five beds accommodating fifty men in a large open space. Each man had about twenty-five square feet of space, including his bunk. A foot locker was at the end of each bed, and at the head of the bed were two stacked lockers for storing additional clothing and uniforms. The floor was a light pine, and there must have been as many windows as bunks, but not one of them had any shades or blinds.

At the front end of the room, by the front doors, were two private rooms where the sergeants and the corporal would be staying during their training. In the back was the latrine. There were a dozen or so showers and thirty-two sinks located on two walls, sixteen on each side with mirrors and of course toilets all lined up in a row. Outside and along the north wall was the furnace and a trap that held the coal. Each night, there would be a fire watch posted and stood by some soldier from that barracks. In the winter, their main concern was to shovel coal in the furnace and keep the heat in the room. Now in the event there was a fire, their job was to alert the men and get them out safely. There was evidence of fire in the past, probably because someone stoked the fire too much, and the evidence was a skeleton of a former barracks standing like a shadow hiding across the street.

All the way in the back, just outside the latrine was a single screen door that squeaks loudly when you opened it and slammed even louder when you went through it. Once out the door, two steps down led you to an open field where the men would spend a lot of their time doing close-order drills, exercising, training, and in the evening, just relaxing while having a smoke. It wasn't much to write home about, but Jim was trying his best to put down what he saw in words so Anna would know where he was, what it was like and mostly to assure her that he was doing just fine and hoping she was doing the same.

After all the men had settled in, Jim noticed a group of them gathering by Ray's bunk. It appeared Ray had enticed a few of them in a game of craps. Now Jim wasn't a gambler; he figured he worked too hard for his money. Still he had an interest in the action, at least to watch. Just as Jim started to walk toward Ray's bunk, Corporal Mitchell walked in and turned over the bunk by Ray.

"Just where in the hell do you think you are?" he asked.

Ray looked at the corporal and said, "I guess you're as much against a man gambling as that first sergeant is against good cigars."

Well, you can figure who stood the first fire watch that night. In fact, Ray would become a regular at that watch during his stay at Fort Worden.

"Lights out," yelled the corporal as each man climbed into his bunk. Jim looked out the window at the full moon and wondered if Anna could see it from her bedroom back in Iowa. A long day had finally come to an end, and tomorrow, a new beginning awaited him. Jim saw the man sitting on the bunk next to him and realized they had not met and that this was the same man who got on the train with him from Camp Dodge. He thought about saying something but then realized there wasn't much time to start a conversation, and since his bunk was next to his, he would find time in the next twelve weeks to get to know him. For now, time to get some sleep because the one thing Jim had already learned about this man's army is they like to get up early.

(from left to right) My uncle, Jim Mitchell; Grandma Phoebe; and Grandpa James Mitchell

Chapter 7

BECOMING ONE

Basic training is just that, training every person regardless of his or her military occupational specialty must go through. It is this training that lies at the very foundation of any effective fighting force and every soldier, sailor, marine, and airman has to pass through it to earn his or her uniform. The primary purpose of this training is to strip them from their civilian habits and establish a new routine. It helps each recruit to meet the requirements for daily life in the military and gives those, who can meet the demands of this training, a new appreciation for their own capabilities. Basic is broken down into five areas. First is fitness. The demanding physical regimen is essential to mold recruits both mentally and physically. This training prepares the recruit to be able to survive the demands of combat and gives them the survival skills they will need in combat. The daily exercise routine helps promote the necessary coordination, cardiovascular fitness, and mental discipline they will need.

Second is military knowledge. Basic trainees learn the skills common to all military members: how to handle weapons, basic first aid, marching, military courtesy, and terminology. Recruits are taught how to maintain themselves, their uniforms, and equipment to a high standard, instilling both pride and knowledge.

Third is esprit de corps. These recruits join a closed community that provides them with a common experience they will share with those who came before them and with those who will follow, becoming part of something, with a long and proud history and a mission greater than any individual. Basic training instills pride in the effort it takes to become a "veteran" and the appreciation for the history and customs of military service.

Fourth is teamwork. Teamwork is essential within the basic platoon and recruits' bond with their fellow servicemen, learning to work, move, and live together under rules that see only "green," never black, white, or any other color. They must learn to discard their individual concerns for the sake of the greater mission as well as the requirement for them to work together to achieve that mission.

Fifth is discipline. Soldiers must learn to not only understand spoken commands but also obey them without question or without thought. There will never be a recruit who likes getting woke at "o'dark thirty" to go marching around in the rain toting a heavy pack, but it is then when they can get out the door in the proper uniform in the time allocated and manage the load without thought of the conditions to get the job done. When they don't have to stop and remember what a particular order means, then they earn the right to be called a soldier.

* * * *

It was four thirty in the morning when the lights went on, and Corporal Mitchell started slamming a wooden baton inside an empty metal trash can, yelling, "Get up! You have fifteen minutes to be dressed and outside and on the parade field for PT."

Each man sprang from his bed and scrambled to follow the command, tripping over footlockers, stubbing toes on the end of the metal bunks, and trying to not be the last man out of the barracks. They quickly dressed in what they thought was the appropriate attire for PT and went

IN OUR RIGHTEOUS MIGHT

out the back door slamming it behind them. Standing in the middle of the field was Tech Sergeant Henderson, Sergeant Lee, and of course, Corporal Mitchell. The headlights from three deuce-and-halfs lit up the parade field. Jim saw that each man was dressed in OD green trousers, unbloused, a white T-shirt, and boots.

"Fall in," commanded Sergeant Lee. He went on to say, "Each morning you will fall out in this formation on this parade field dressed just like me." As he was speaking, Corporal Mitchell was marking four spots on the parade field, indicating they would be separated into four squads.

Sergeant Lee said, "The first name I call will fall in on the spot Corporal Mitchell has marked on the ground. As your name is called, you will stand on that spot, and you will assume the position of acting squad leader. There are four squads and those will make up a platoon known as the second platoon of the Company C training division."

One by one, Corporal Mitchell and Tech Sergeant Henderson called out the names of the men and placed them in a spot within a squad. Jim was in the second squad of the platoon and was in the first position, indicating he was going to be the squad leader. Now Jim knew nothing about being a squad leader and wondered just how his name was selected. He wanted to ask but then remembered the last time he asked a question back at Camp Dodge to the sergeant major and decided he would remain silent.

Once each man was assigned a position, the sergeant said, "Men, look to your left, now to your right, and learn the name of that man. That is who will be standing next to you every time we are in formation."

After some instructions on how to line themselves up, they spread themselves so they could exercise without hitting each other. The physical training started with stretches and calisthenics and finally finished with a short two-mile run. Once back at their barracks, they were dismissed to prepare themselves for the day. They had thirty minutes to shit, shower, shave, make their bunks, and be in formation to march over for breakfast.

With only twelve showers, it was going to take the men a few days to realize that not everyone could shower at the same time. They would learn that while some were showering, others could be shaving or making their bunks, straightening out their space, or putting another coat of polish on their boots. Some would choose to shower once the lights went out so they would have more time in the morning.

There wasn't a day that went by in the first three weeks that a fight didn't break out because someone was using too much time in the shower, leaving less or no time at all for the others. They learned that a shower wasn't the only thing limited—so was the amount of hot water that was available. In order to conserve, the men had to turn on the water, wet down, shut the water off, soap up, and then turn the water on one more time to rinse.

Each morning after breakfast, they would return to the barracks where they were given time to clean and prepare their quarters for inspection. Like all new recruits, they failed miserably, which resulted in extended marching, additional time on the parade field doing calisthenics, or if they really screwed up, the beloved ten-mile hike.

Individuals failing to comply with the set standards would find the consequences to be somewhat harsh. For instance, a bunk not made tight enough to bounce a coin on would be turned over on the floor. The untidy footlockers would find the contents scattered on the floor. And not being properly shaved would find a soldier standing in formation dry shaving.

In the military, if one man failed the inspection, the entire barracks failed the inspection. On several occasions, this mass punishment led to some very hard feelings, and a few fights broke out that the squad leader had to halt. On one occasion, the men were standing at ease on the parade field while Sergeant Lee and Corporal Mitchell were inside conducting their morning inspection of the barracks. All of a sudden, Sergeant Lee came out and told the first squad leader to fall out and follow him inside the barracks. Unknown to anyone, apparently someone had taken a shit and did not flush. The first squad leader had to remove the turd from the toilet with his hands, take it out to the formation, and pass it down to each member of his squad. This was repeated until it came to the last man of the fourth squad who ran back into the barracks and flushed. Things like this would leave a lasting impression on every man. So before the last man fell in for inspection each morning, someone, probably more than one, walked by all the toilets.

After inspections were completed, they continued their day learning to become soldiers. This included time on the rifle range where they became proficient with the M1 carbine. This was a lightweight, easy-to-use, semi-automatic rifle that could be fired from the hip. It would become the standard firearm for the U.S. military during World War II. Each soldier was expected to become proficient with this weapon. They were taught every aspect from how it worked, how to break it down for cleaning, and how to clear jams quickly. They would learn to break the carbine down and reassemble it so many times they could have done it in their sleep. They went to the firing range at least three times a week where they would fire this weapon from ranges of seventy-five to three hundred meters. In order to get through Basic and move on, each soldier had to qualify at the minimum of "marksman" before they graduated. Not graduating didn't mean going home; it meant being recycled and getting to repeat Basic again— something no man wanted.

It was on the grenade-throwing range where the men learned the deadly consequences of the war and the equipment they would be using to wage it. The Mark 2 defensive hand grenade (sometimes written Mark II) is a fragmentation hand grenade, and the men were being taught the correct procedure for throwing it. The sergeant who was conducting the exercise was in a foxhole with two of the recruits. One by one, each man was shown the proper way to hold the grenade, pull the pin, and throw it.

As the two recruits, not from Jim's squad, were preparing to throw the grenade, one of them dropped it in the foxhole.

The sergeant immediately yelled "grenade!" and quickly threw the two recruits out. Just as the last one rolled away, the grenade exploded, killing the sergeant. A medic immediately entered the foxhole and realized the sergeant was dead, covering him up using his poncho. The first sergeant came over, looked down into the foxhole, and told the medic to remove the cover. One by one, each man was directed past the dead sergeant. They were to look in and see what the consequences of carelessness can do.

Jim had never seen a dead man before and certainly had never seen someone killed. The shrapnel from the grenade had penetrated the sergeant's throat as well as his stomach exposing his large intestines. Blood was pouring from the wound in his neck and was slowly soaking the dirt by his head. The sight of the lifeless body made Jim throw up in his mouth. As each man filed by, they became keenly aware of their new profession and the results of what can happen to them, which was exactly why the first sergeant ordered them to look. It was a tragedy that, according to the first sergeant, needed to be viewed so it wouldn't be repeated.

Jim sat on his bunk thinking of the young sergeant who was killed. He wondered what he would have done if he were in the sergeant's shoes. Would he have thrown the other men out first, or would he have jumped out of the fox hole?

A voice came from behind him and said, "I don't know if I could have been that brave."

Jim looked up and saw the man who rode from Camp Dodge with him and said, "I hope I will never have to make that decision."

The man stuck out his hand and said, "My name is Leonard Davidson, and I'm from Batavia, Iowa."

Leonard was a small man, standing about five feet eight with dark brown hair and hazel eyes. As they shook hands, Jim couldn't help but notice how soft his hands were, indicating he probably wasn't a farmer. Jim introduced himself and said he too was from Iowa and asked what Leonard had done before joining the army.

"I worked in a bank as a bookkeeper and was hoping to become a loan officer, but then the war came knocking."

"So I take it you didn't volunteer for this assignment?" Jim inquired. Leonard immediately responded, "Well, I was thinking about what I wanted to do it but then came the letter, and the decision was made. How about you?"

Jim said, "I hear you. I was going to join the navy with my father-in-law and my brother-in-law, but those plans were changed. So Leonard, did you leave a wife back home?"

"No, not yet. I guess I spent too much time in the bank and never got around to that. I figure when this is over, I might find room for both my career and a family," Leonard responded. And then he said, "Jim, you can call me Lad, all my friends do."

Jim smiled and said, "Well, according to Private Mansini, you can call me Arky, as he seems to think I am a baseball player."

Lad looked over at Jim and said, "I do see the resemblance, but I don't think someone hitting .312 would be in the army."

Both men talked a while before the lights went off ending another day.

Sunday was a day the men would enjoy since week six of their training. It was this day that there was little if any training and morning chow was optional. There were no inspections, no forced marches or PT, and the only thing that was not optional was attending church services. Every man would attend some service depending on his religious preference. You were expected to be in dress uniform sitting at attention in the pew, and God help the soldier who nodded off to sleep. Sleepers would find themselves guarding the clothesline the rest of the day in full combat gear, including a weapon. The primary purpose for this watch was to prevent someone from helping themselves to uniforms that were already laundered and did not belong to them, leaving theirs behind.

It was two weeks ago, and one of the men in Jim's squad, J.M. Larson, who hailed from Duluth, Minnesota, was caught sleeping through services and of course was moved to the clothesline for his punishment. While he was standing that watch, Corporal Mitchell approached and started asking him questions about the general orders for the watch he was on. Larson recited the orders to the satisfaction of the corporal who then asked if the private needed anything. Larson responded he could use a break to go to the latrine. The corporal said he could go, but he was to be quick about it. As Larson started to leave, he asked the corporal if he could watch his "gun." Now your rifle was like your best friend. You never abandoned it, never shared it, and never called it a "gun." A lesson the private, along with the rest of the recruits, would soon learn.

At chow that day, Private Larson was ordered to run around inside the chow hall, while the other soldiers ate with his rifle in one hand and his penis in the other. He would yell, "This is my weapon, and this is my gun. One is for shooting, one is for fun."

This went on for just a few minutes and was abruptly halted when the post chaplain came in and put a stop to it. He looked at Corporal Mitchell and said, "I think you have made your point, corporal, don't you?"

Jim thought of the humiliation for the young man and how he, as his squad leader, would need to approach him later in the day to unruffle his feathers. He had become rather effective in approaching the men and getting them to laugh about whatever their punishment that had been handed out. Many soldiers had to sleep with their weapon because they dropped it, mistreated it, or started to walk away from it.

Jim recalled the day Lad Davidson was standing in formation after they had all eaten, having a pipe when all of a sudden, the mess sergeant came out madder than hell and pointed to him. Lad was summoned to the front of the platoon where the mess sergeant stated that when Private Davidson exited the Mess Hall, he splashed the sergeant with dirty dishwater when he tossed his silverware in the pan. Lad's punishment was to have the mess sergeant dump that same pan of dirt dishwater over his head.

Jim never really understood the types of punishment used but saw the effect they had, not only on the man being punished but on everyone else too. Once you received the wrath of Sergeant Lee for screwing up, you could expect to receive additional training, as he liked to call it. That training could be demonstrating the proper technique of digging a two-man foxhole only to fill it in again, pushing rocks one rock at a time off the sidewalk with a tooth brush, and running around the formation with your weapon overhead or push-ups. How he loved to dish out push-ups. The recruits didn't understand at the time of the reasoning, but it was a tool used to instill unity, teamwork, and obedience—the kind of obedience that would be needed in combat. They would be expected to follow their leaders without question, regardless of the danger or conditions. It was this training that would make them soldiers ready to face the worst man and machine had to offer.

Most of the men were sitting around the barracks, either catching up on lost sleep, writing letters, or trying to get a shine back on their boots when two military policemen walked in and down the path toward the corporal's office. They watched as the MPs entered, and in a few minutes, they heard Corporal Mitchell yell for Private Mansini to come to his office.

Ray, who was playing cards and smoking a cigar, got up, said something to the men, and strolled to the office. It wasn't long before the MPs reappeared with Ray in hand. His hands were cuffed behind his back, and each MP had an arm as they led him past the platoon, down the corridor, and out the back door. Confused and in disbelief, the men looked around to see if anyone understood what was going on.

Sergeant Lee stepped out on the floor and ordered all the squad leaders to report immediately to his office. As Jim and the others stepped through the door, they were greeted by a captain who introduced himself as Captain Hagg from the JAG's office. Captain Hagg told the men to stand at ease and then proceeded to give the details as to why Private Ray Mansini was taken out of the barracks in handcuffs. It seemed that Mansini was, at the time of his enlistment, wanted in connection with some book-making charges in Chicago, and his lawyer tried to hide him in the military, thinking the prosecution would then drop any charges they had.

Jim immediately recalled the conversation he had with Mansini when they first met on the train. Ray was right; his father and lawyer were trying to pull a fast one. The fast one wasn't on Ray but on the local police by getting him out of town and out of sight.

Captain Hagg informed the squad leaders that they could tell the members of their squad just what he had told them and nothing more. They were to remember to hold any judgment and let the courts and the military decide on Private Mansini's future. With that being said, they were dismissed.

* * * *

Those who went off to fight in this war weren't the only ones who were faced with change and adversity. So were those left at home. In May of 1942, the U.S. Government introduced rationing, placing a freeze on practically all everyday goods starting with sugar, coffee, and tires. Gasoline was rationed, not because there was a shortage but as a way to curb driving and wear on the tires so they would last longer.

Most of the rubber trees were found in the South Pacific, and those trees were currently in the hands of the Japanese. They would need the rubber to produce masks, tires, gaskets, and other items to fight this war; so limiting gasoline to save the need for rubber was crucial to the effort. War-ration books with tokens were issued to each American family, dictating how much gasoline, tires, sugar, meat, silk, shoes, nylon, and other items any person could buy. Tires, cars, bicycles, gasoline, fuel oil and kerosene, solid fuels, stoves, rubber footwear, shoes, sugar, coffee, processed foods, meats, canned fish cheese, canned milk, fats, and even typewriters were on the list of products to be rationed. The federal government needed to control supply and demand. And to avoid anger and resentment for those with money and influence, they introduced rationing books with stamps that had an expiration date. The amount a family would be allowed to have was based on the size of the family, not the amount of money one had. The coupon book provided the holder with a set amount that they could use to purchase items for that family. Registration usually took place in local schools where one member of the family would register all the members of their family, giving ages and a description so a fair portion would be allocated.

Each stamp authorized a purchase of rationed goods in the quantity and time designated, which guaranteed that the family had its fair share of goods.

The coupon book came with specifications and deadlines so one could not save for next time. Rationing, of course, brought opportunity for some through the black market where people could buy rationed items on the sly at much higher prices. For the most part, black marketers dealt meat, sugar, and gasoline. The familiar blue box of Kraft Macaroni and Cheese Dinner became popular as a substitute for meat and dairy products. Two boxes required only one rationing coupon. Food substitutions became into play where things like real butter was replaced with oleomargarine or lard. Americans didn't mind the sacrifice as long as it was fair because they knew the boys overseas needed it more than they did.

* * * *

Anna was feeling the burden of trying to keep the house on what she was making at the phone company and that which Jim could send home. The army paid considerably less than what Jim was making at the dairy, which created a budget shortfall some months. She also worried about her mother who would soon be alone now that her father and brother had enlisted in the navy and were awaiting their orders. She had written to Jim about her concerns, and he agreed it might be best if she moved back home with her mother. By doing this, they would not only be able to look after each other, but also they could make their money go a little further; and by combining their rations books, they would have more points to purchase items on the ration list.

Art stopped and picked Anna up so she could go discuss the idea of her moving back in with her mom and dad. Anna was hoping Doc Wagner would allow her to store their furniture in the barn until she could figure out what to do. She assumed the car could be placed up on blocks at her father's house, seeing she had no use for the vehicle because neither she nor her mother had ever learned to drive or get a driver's license. Art pulled up in the drive and honked. Anna grabbed her purse, along with an umbrella, as it looked like rain was coming, and headed out the door.

Once in the car, Art said, "So, Sis, what's up? I hear you need to talk to Dad and Mom?"

Anna looked over at her brother, patted him on the arm, and said, "Oh, nothing much. Just wanted to discuss plans with Mom now that you men are abandoning us girls."

As they pulled into the driveway, the skies opened up, and down came the rain. A clap of thunder rolled through the clouds shaking the car and startling Anna. She opened the door and the umbrella and ran to the house, leaving Art to fend for himself. Craig was sitting on the porch in the big swing smoking a cigarette as Anna came up on the porch.

"Hello, Dad," Anna said as she shook the umbrella out and put it away. "Sure not much of a night to be sitting on the porch," Art said as he came up on the porch.

"Nonsense," said Craig, "it is just a little Iowa storm, and we need the rain. I am under cover, and I enjoy watching the clouds move by."

The door opened, and Mary came out on the porch joining Craig in the swing.

"So I hear you want to discuss the future without the men," Mary said. Anna stated her case, explaining her plan of moving back home, and

now waited for her parents to respond. Craig only said her plan was well thought out and very thoughtful. Mary, on the other hand, didn't see the need to combine.

She said, "Now you have made your bed, and you need to sleep in it. I was just fine when your father went overseas for World War I, and both of us will be just fine for this one. You two have worked too hard to give up that house. Besides, Jim needs to know that his world, at least back here, is the same."

Craig spoke up telling Anna she should sell the car. "Even with rationing, you should be able to get a good price, and that money should be enough to pay the rent for a year or so. I really believe by that time this should be over and Jim will be back home."

Anna, realizing that there was no reason to pursue the conversation any further, turned and asked Art if he could sell the car.

"No problem, Sis," Art responded, "but shouldn't you write Jim first?" "Oh, I will," answered Anna. "Do either of you have any idea how long before you leave or where you will be going?"

Craig said he figured it would be sometime in September or early October. As to where they would be going, he figured the Great Lakes Naval Training Center outside of Chicago.

Anna went inside to get a cup of coffee when the phone rang. She walked over to the table and answered. She heard Daryl's voice at the other end.

He said, "Anna, I tried your house, and when you didn't answer, I thought you might be with your parents. I am calling from the hospital because Hazel has gone into labor."

Anna paused for a moment and then said, "Isn't this early? I thought she had another four weeks?"

Daryl explained, "She does, but when we were downtown this afternoon, a child came running around the corner, hitting her, and knocking her off her feet. A few minutes later, she started labor or so they have said. The doctors are with her now."

Anna hung up the telephone and went outside, telling everyone what had happened. She looked to Art and asked if he could take her to the hospital.

The rain had stopped but not the thunder. Art and Anna said goodbye to their parents and headed to the car.

Anna arrived at the hospital and went through the large glass doors over to the receptionist desk where a young nun was sitting. She told her who she was looking for and asked if she could give her direction to the delivery waiting area. She was directed to the elevator that would take her to the fourth floor. As she exited the elevator, she turned to her left and saw Daryl smoking a cigarette and pacing the floor. John and Martha, Hazel's parents, were also there sitting motionless looking off into the distance.

Daryl looked very different from the last time she had seen him as he stood there in his uniform smoking a cigarette. Anna went over and gave him a hug, introduced her brother, and asked if he knew anything.

"No," Daryl said, "she has been in there for a little over three hours now, and the only thing I know is the doctor is with her."

Art asked if anyone could use anything from the café.

"I could use a cup of coffee and so could Daryl, if you don't mind," said Anna.

"If they have any Pall Mall cigarettes, I could use another pack," Daryl said as he pulled out a one-dollar bill and handed it to Art. Anna directed Daryl over to a large brown sofa where they both sat and waited.

It was a little after midnight when the doctor came out and went over to Daryl. He signaled for him to remain seated as he pulled up a chair and said that Hazel was having a difficult time because she was not dilating enough for the baby to be born. He needed Daryl's consent to take her to surgery where they could do a cesarean section and deliver the baby.

Daryl looked to Hazel's mom, who shook her head in approval, and said, "Yes, whatever you need to do, please do."

The doctor told Daryl that he could go see his wife for a few minutes while he and the nurses got the surgical room setup. Daryl, Anna, and Mrs. Roberts went to see Hazel.

She looked pale but had a smile on her face as she reached out for Daryl's hand and said, "Well, are you ready to be a daddy?"

Daryl squeezed her hand and said he was and asked how she was doing. Hazel must have seen concern on Anna's face, so she said, "Oh, Anna, I am going to be fine as soon as I pass this bowling ball."

As Hazel and her mother were exchanging small talk, a nurse came into the room and asked if everyone could go back to the waiting area as it was time to take Hazel to the surgical unit.

The nurse came over to the bed, wiped Hazel's forehead, and asked, "Are you ready?"

Hazel nodded her head yes as Daryl bent down and kissed her.

"I will be right here when you get back with our child," said Daryl. Once the surgery was completed, Hazel was taken to the recovery room, and the baby was taken to the nursery. The doctor came out and told Daryl that the surgery went well and that Hazel was just fine. The doctor went on to tell Daryl their son was born too premature and that his lungs were not fully developed. He did not believe the child could live more than a few hours, and they were doing all they could for him and to keep him comfortable.

Daryl asked, "Does Hazel know?"

"No, she is still heavily sedated from the anesthesia. Would you like to go to the nursery and hold your son?" the doctor asked.

Daryl quietly followed the nurse to the nursery where he could say hello and goodbye to his son. Once in the room, the nurse handed him this very small child wrapped in a soft white blanket. Daryl examined him seeing the tiny features that seemed to be so perfect on the outside. But it wasn't the same on the inside. He felt the heartbreak that only a father could feel knowing this moment would be too brief. As tears swelled in his eyes, he bent down and kissed his son on the head. Daryl sat in the nursery just quietly holding him in his arms and rocking. His thoughts were on how unfair this was, that this would be his memory of his son and all their tomorrows would be over in a couple of hours. He wept for his wife and the realization that he had to break the news to her.

Anna told Art he could leave but that she wanted to stay with Hazel and was sure that either Daryl or Hazel's parents would bring her home.

Art gave his sister a big hug and said, "I am sorry, Sis, I know how much you are hurting for your friend."

Anna walked over to the fourth floor window and gazed out catching the first signs of morning breaking through the clouds. The raindrops were sliding down the window like the tears that were sliding down Anna's cheeks. Her thoughts were with both Hazel and with Jim and how she wished he could be there holding her. Anna recalled the conversation when John was putting together the crib and how Martha warned of it being a sign of bad luck. Anna wondered, "How do they know this?" She reached inside her purse and found a handkerchief to wipe the tears from her eyes as she slowly walked back to the bench to sit with Martha and John and wait for Hazel to wake up.

Chapter 8

CHANGE IN PLANS

The last few days, each platoon had spent three to four hours marching, listening to cadence, following commands, and drilling, so they reacted and moved as one unit. It was the first of July, and Jim's platoon had joined up with the other four, which made up their training command in preparation for the parade they would be attending in Seattle. It would be their first venture away from the base since their arrival and their first opportunity to demonstrate their readiness to the American public. Jim, like all the other troops, was excited to get off the base and maybe relax a little. But his joy was also tampered by a little sadness knowing that this wasn't how he envisioned he would spend his first anniversary with Anna.

As Jim was brushing the final shine on his boots, Lad came over to his bunk.

"Hey, Arky, did you see the *Stars and Stripes* today?"

Jim looked up and saw Davidson approaching with a newspaper in hand. As Lad sat down, he handed the paper over to Jim who glanced over the headline which revealed that the navy had won a very decisive victory at Coral Sea and Midway, two small islands in the Pacific. The importance of the island was the air base, and whoever controlled that small island also controlled the airfield which could be used to launch attacks against other islands as well as naval ships.

Jim smiled when he read that the U.S. Navy had destroyed or sunk four of the aircraft carriers that were used to attack Pearl Harbor.

"So what do you think, Jim?" Lad asked.

"I am not sure. It is obviously a good win, but there are still a lot of islands to contend with."

Lad agreed and said, "But I really don't see why we are going to be needed here as coastal artillery now that the Jap's ability to strike has been crippled. I am thinking we are either going to join the fight in the Pacific or we are going, which makes more since, to get moved to the European theater."

Looking at Davidson's face, Jim paused and said, "I think you may be on to something, but remember you did say it made sense, so who knows?"

They both laughed as Sergeant Lee entered the barracks yelling, "Okay, men, fall out on the parade field. Let's get back to making you look like soldiers before Saturday's parade."

The bus ride down to Seattle took about three hours as they drove the windy roads down the coastline. Jim enjoyed seeing the ocean and wondered if those who see it all the time ever take its magnificence for granted. It was still early enough that Jim couldn't see the horizon because of the fog and knew the same would be true when they returned, as it would be dark. The men were told that after the parade, they would have the rest of the day to themselves to do as they wished. They were warned to stay out of the bars, away from any whore houses that might be present, and to be on their very best behavior. If they were going to buy something, they had to ship it home. There would be military police patrolling the area, and getting into trouble would more than likely result in being recycled through basic, which would be tragic, seeing that they only had three weeks until the end.

Jim had only two things on his mind. He just wanted to find a phone to call Anna so he could hear her voice and wish her a happy anniversary. After that, he wanted to go into a restaurant, sit down, and eat without being in a hurry and have a good old-fashioned Fourth of July dinner. A meal with fried chicken, potato salad, and maybe some barbecue beans; no sense wishing for some Iowa sweet corn. He then would top it off with some ice-cold watermelon for dessert along with a bottle of soda.

When the buses finally arrived at the assembly area and parked, the men quickly got off and fell into formation. As they stood silently looking around, there was a loud command of "attention!" All the men quickly responded with their eyes straightforward and hands straight down by their side. Out-front of the formation, a lieutenant colonel came into view. He stood before them in his sharply pressed dress uniform with a saber hanging from his right side.

"Men, Today, I have the privilege of marching in this parade with you. I want each one of you to remember that you not only represent yourself but that you represent the United States Army and its proud tradition and heritage dating all the way back to 1775. Remember those civilians who will be lining the parade route will be watching you. They are still a little scared and unsure of what is going to happen in the months and maybe years to come. We can assure them that they have nothing to fear because we are willing to take this fight to our enemies by demonstrating our professionalism and our readiness in how we conduct ourselves today."

With that said, he turned, saluted the lieutenant, and walked away.

"Stand at ease" came the command from First Sergeant Fisher.

The skies were a little overcast, but the chance of rain was minimal. In fact, even with all the rain Seattle gets each year, July was on average the driest month of the entire year. There was a very slight breeze coming in from the coast, keeping temperatures in the mid seventies and making it a perfect day for the one-mile march they would make for the parade.

The company had no problem with this march, and the crowds seemed to be very enthusiastic, waving flags and cheering as they came by. Once the company had made the corner and reached the end of the parade route, First Sergeant Fisher informed them that they were to be in that exact same location at 1800 hours for the return trip back to the base. He again reminded them of the out-of-bound areas and what they could expect for those who failed to follow instructions.

Jim, Lad, and Otto Merringer—a young man from Moline, Illinois, who in civilian life worked as a clown with the Barnum and Bailey Circus, all started the walk back into town. As they walked, they saw soldiers, sailors, and marines everywhere. There were hot dog stands, vendors selling roasted peanuts, fresh popcorn, and girls everywhere, hoping to catch the eye of a serviceman. Every time Jim saw a pay phone, he also saw a line waiting to use it. He hoped as the day grew into the afternoon, a phone would become available.

As they came up to a bus stop, an older couple approached introducing themselves and then invited the men to come to their home for a Fourth of July dinner. They said that they wanted to thank the servicemen by providing an enjoyable afternoon where they could relax and for a few hours forget about the military. Their names were Gladys and Harry Granger who said they had a son serving in the U.S. Navy. They had prepared a lot of food in hopes they could entertain a few of the servicemen who came to Seattle today. They asked if the three of them, as well as two marines who were also standing at the bus stop, could please indulge a couple of older people who had only their hospitality to offer the war effort. Jim, Lad, and Otto, and the marines climbed in the back of their pickup.

After a short drive through town and out a couple of miles, the truck turned down a dirt road that was lined by mature maple trees that draped over the road like a roof over a house. The road led to a circle driveway where the truck stopped in front of a very large two-story house. The front yard was well-groomed with a stone walkway leading up to the front porch. On both sides of the porch were two round bushes that had a simple and very small red flower blooming. There were black shutters on each window, and the house looked like it had just received a fresh coat of white paint. As they walked through the front door, they were taken through the library to the sitting room where they were told they could leave their coats, hats, leggings, and ties. Lad noticed a photo of a young man in a naval uniform standing on a battleship. He looked to Jim and said, "Jim, look at this picture. Doesn't that look like Hawaii to you?"

Jim said, "Well, I have never been to Hawaii but from all I have seen in magazines and heard, I would say you are right."

Just then, Mrs. Granger entered the room and said, "Oh, that is a photo of our son Raymond. He sent it to us last November when his ship, the USS *Arizona*, arrived in Honolulu."

She noticed the look on their faces and said, "Yes, he was on the ship the day the Japanese attacked, but somehow he was spared. He is currently in the hospital recovering from his wounds and burns to his back and arms. But he is fine, and we are hoping he can make it home soon."

Otto, not sure what to say, just walked over to Mrs. Granger, gave her a hug, and said, "I am sure he is as excited to see you as you are him, and I hope it will be soon."

They followed Mrs. Granger through the kitchen and out to the backyard. As they went through the screen door, they saw a very large yard leading to a cliff that overlooked Puget Sound. The sun was now shining, and the water glistened as the sailboats slowly made their way through the waters. There were so many trees in the backyard, mostly apples, that it made it difficult to see the end of the property line. Each of the trees was keeping pace with the breeze as the white billowing clouds slid by like they were sailing themselves on the blue skies. There was a large deck that came off the second-floor master bedroom, providing an incredible view of the surrounding area. The chairs and small table on the deck were evidence that Gladys and Raymond spent many evenings just enjoying their good fortune. Under that deck was a door that came from the kitchen where there were two tables set up with checkered tablecloths waiting to accommodate their guests.

Raymond came over to the men, who were standing looking out at the sound, and handed each a hand-rolled cigar. He explained each point of interest they saw and pointed to the docks where so many boats were docked. These were the boats his company used for commercial fishing. Fishing had been in the family business for eighty years, and he, like his father before him, would be handing the business over to his son once this war was over. Just as they were lighting their cigars, Mrs. Granger called the boys to come to the table for dinner.

Raymond looked back in and said, "Maybe we should enjoy these after dinner. Shall we eat?"

They sat down to a meal of fried chicken, corn on the cob, potato salad, baked beans, and for dessert, there was homemade ice cream and, of course, apple pie. Jim enjoyed a cold bottle of cream soda, and Lad and Otto chose a cold beer. As they ate, the conversation turned to their home, and Jim revealed that today was his first wedding anniversary and that he was hoping he would be able to call Anna sometime before they headed back to the bus. Mrs. Granger immediately spoke up saying she insisted he use the phone in the den to call home as soon as dinner was over.

Jim said he would reverse the charges, but Raymond would have none of that, saying, "You talk as long as you wish, son, it is the least we can do for our boys in uniform."

After dinner, Jim was escorted to the den where he was left alone to call Anna. He first tried the house, and after several rings, he realized that Anna was probably enjoying the day with her parents.

The phone rang several times before a familiar voice answered. It was Art.

"Hello, Jim," he said. "I suppose you are calling to talk to Anna, but she isn't here."

"Oh, Art, give me that phone." Jim heard Anna's voice in the background as she reached for the phone.

In Jim's pocket was a photo of Anna he carried wherever he went. He removed the photo as a reminder of how beautiful she was and as a reminder of how lucky he was to have her in his life.

"Hi, Jim, how are you? Where are you?" asked Anna.

They talked for several minutes as Jim explained where he was and the kindness of the family he was spending the day with. Anna assured him all was well at home and that everyone was good. Toward the end of the conversation and right before they were to say goodbye, Anna said, "Jim, I will be thinking of you tonight and about our wedding day a year ago."

Jim replied, "Well, if you do, you're not going to get much sleep."

"Oh, Jim, I see nothing has changed. You're still impossible. I love you very much, and I can't wait to see you," Anna replied.

It was hard saying goodbye, but Jim didn't want to run up the phone bill and was so grateful to actually have had the chance to hear her voice.

After Jim hung up, he walked out of the den through the kitchen and out to the patio where the men were eating their dessert.

"Everything good on the home front, old man?" asked Otto.

Jim nodded his head as Mrs. Granger placed a very large piece of apple pie with two scoops of ice cream in front of him.

It was 5:15, and even though they didn't want to say goodbye, they knew it was time to go. They thanked the Grangers for their hospitality as they loaded back into the pickup to go back into town where the buses were waiting to take them back to their reality. As they drove down the long driveway, Jim glanced back to see Mrs. Granger wiping her eyes with a white handkerchief. He thought of their kindness and hoped someday he could introduce Anna to them and pay them back for the day they shared.

Otto spoke up and said, "Can you imagine the view you could have to watch the evening fireworks from their upstairs deck?"

It would have been spectacular, but their only view of any fireworks this year would be through the windows of the bus going back to the base.

All the men were accounted for as they loaded the bus and settled in for the three-hour return trip. It was rumored that a few men, not on their bus but within the company, may have had a few too many beers, and they hoped that those indiscretions would not result in any extra training when they got back. Lad and Otto reached into their pocket and pulled out the cigars Mr. Granger had given them.

"Hey, Sergeant, would it be okay if we smoke these cigars we got?"

"I don't give a damn as long as you put the window down" came the response.

Jim knew he had left his on the table, so he reached for his pipe when he heard "Hey, Arky, would you rather have this?" Lad handed the cigar to him. "I knew you really didn't want to leave this behind, so I took the liberty of taking it for you."

Otto, Jim, and Lad enjoyed the sunset and the satisfaction of a good cigar, while most of the men loosened their ties and nodded off to sleep.

Once back at the camp, the men were dismissed to return to their barracks for one hour of private time before "Taps." Jim lay in his rack thinking of Anna and then chuckled to himself because he knew if he didn't get his mind on something else, he wouldn't be getting any sleep tonight either. Lad was writing a letter when a commotion started in the front of the barracks. "Attention!" came the command.

Each man jumped from his bunk and stood in front of it in whatever form of dress they were in. The battalion commander entered the room and told the men to stand at ease.

"Men, I have some news to share with you, and even though it is late, I believe you need to know what is going on and how it is going to affect you. As you know, the Battle of Bataan was a huge blow to us and our allies in April. Many of our soldiers and sailors have been captured and are being marched deep into the jungles to be held in remote locations. But with the defeat of the Japanese Navy at Midway, we believe we have balanced the power, and we have stopped those bastards cold in their tracks. They are digging in for a fight, but soon they will feel the power of this sleeping giant."

A loud cheer went up in the barracks as the colonel asked for silence. "There is still much to do, and a long fight is before us with no guarantee of the date of our victory, but rest assured victory will be ours. With that being said, our mission here has been reevaluated, and your services are going to be needed elsewhere. With what has transpired, there is very little concern for the need to keep a large number of men guarding our coastline. Your graduation from these training facilities is being moved up, and within four to six days, you will receive a new set of orders taking you to other military locations for training in new MOS's. Some of you will continue in the coastline defense and will be heading to Camp McQuaid, California, but most of you will be heading to Camp Barkeley, located outside of Abilene, Texas, to train on the 155mm howitzer. Along with your orders, you will be given a thirty-day pass to go home and spend some time with your family. You cannot contact your family and reveal any of these plans until you have your orders in hand and have received clearance. For now, this information of your movement is considered classified. Are there any questions?"

The unified answer came loud and clear. "No, Sir!"

With that, the first sergeant called them to attention. Each man rose and remained motionless until the commander left the area.

"As you were" came the response from the first sergeant as he went through the door and out to the parade field.

The lights were going out as each man was mulling over the news and the thought of going home for at least a little while.

As Jim lay in his rack, he heard the distant calling of night time and the official ending of another day with the playing of "Taps." As he listened, he realized that today turned out to be one of the best days he has had in his short military career. He met a great family who shared their home and provided a great meal. He finally got to speak to Anna and now the news he would be going home. He knew it was going to be difficult to get a call into Anna before he left, and he knew that, if he mailed a letter, there would be a good chance he would beat it home.

Lad, who was also in his bunk, asked Jim if he knew the history of "Taps." Jim thought it was a strange question based on what had already transpired this day, but answered no.

"As the story goes, General Butterfield, who was the commander of Northern troops who were camped at Harrison Landing in Virginia, was not pleased with the long-standing tradition of the call for Extinguish Lights, sensing it was too formal and harsh for the day's end. He summoned the brigade bugler, Oliver Wilcox Norton, and asked him to write a new version to honor his men while they rested from the seven days of battle that had just ended. On a quiet night in July 1862 for the first time, the new version of "Taps," as we now know it, sounded. This tune became so popular so fast that it spread to other units of the Union Army, and even the Confederates would adopt it as the official sound ending the day.

"Imagine it was just eighty years ago this month that service members were being serenaded for the first time by that lonely, distant sound only a bugle can make," Lad said. "Eighty years, the same time Mr. Granger's family started their fishing business here in Washington. It is a small world, Jim, and we are becoming a bigger part of it."

Jim was amazed how Lad always seemed to take something so simple like "Taps," tie it together, and make it relevant to what was happening in the world today.

"Taps" ended.

Jim just looked at Lad and said, "Good night, Davidson, I hope wherever my orders take me, they send you along to keep me informed."

"Yeah, you're okay too, Arky," Davidson said, as he rolled over in his bunk and pulled the covers over his feet.

Chapter 9

A BRIEF HOMECOMING

Jim's train arrived at the depot at twelve thirty in the afternoon, and he looked around to see if his letter had beaten him home. Realizing it hadn't happened, he found his duffel bag, threw it over his shoulder, and headed to the curb to wait for a taxi. He knew Anna couldn't drive, and his dad, Craig, and Art would be at work so he hailed a cab and took the short ride home. He couldn't wait to see Anna's face when she realized he was home. Oh, she would pretend to be angry and probably make some reference to how she looked but Jim didn't care because he knew she would be the best thing he had seen since he left so many months ago.

The cab turned on his street, and he asked the driver to stop short of the house so he could walk the last few feet. He reached in his pocket, pulled out two dollars, and thanked the driver for the lift. As he approached the house, he could hear Anna in the backyard singing as she was hanging up the washing she had apparently been working on. He gently laid his duffel bag down—as not to startle her—and watched as she hung up each sheet. She had on a soft blue printed cotton dress that moved with the breeze that was blowing on this hot July day. Her hair was back, and she wore a bright yellow scarf over her head to keep the sweat from dripping on her brow. Jim could see small beads of sweat on her neck as she stopped and stretched her back before bending over to grab some more sheets to hang up. He stepped back because he wasn't ready to reveal himself.

He heard the bell on the bike of the mailman out by the box, and it gave him an idea. He grabbed his duffel bag and hurried to catch the mailman to see if he might have the letter he had written. The carrier started to speak, but Jim placed his finger to his mouth signaling for him not to speak. He asked if he could see the mail, and the carrier handed it to him. Sure enough, the letter he sent had arrived. He asked the mailman if he could help him surprise his wife by summoning her to the mailbox telling her he had a special delivery she need to sign for. The mailman played along, yelling, "Mrs. McManis, I will need you to sign for this letter if you will."

Anna wiped her hands on her dress and came around the corner only to see Jim leaning against the mailbox with the letter in his hand. She stopped dead in her tracks and then came running, almost knocking Jim over. They hugged and kissed as the mailman tipped his hat and said, "Enjoy your delivery."

"Jim, what are you doing here?" she asked. "Are you okay? Why didn't you write and tell me you were coming home? I must look a fright."

Jim kissed her again and said, "First, I did write, and here is the letter, and second, you will never look anything but beautiful as far as I am concerned. Now you can open the letter, or if you want, we can go inside, and I can tell what the letter says."

They went inside, but the letter never did get opened.

Later, Jim was sitting in his favorite chair on the front porch, enjoying his pipe, and watching the sunset finally bring an end to this hot and sticky summer's day. He could hear Anna in the kitchen cleaning up from supper when she called to him asking if he would like a cold beer or a glass of ice tea.

"What are you having?" asked Jim.

"I think iced tea for me" was her response. Jim said that would be fine for him as well. She soon joined Jim on the porch, and together they sat and watched the lightning bugs fly around the yard lighting their tail as if they were small little flashlights. Jim looked over to the window and saw a small cloth hanging in the window. It was about the size of a pack of cigarettes, and the outside was trimmed in red on a white cloth with a blue star in the middle.

"Anna, what is that hanging in the window?" Jim asked.

"That is something we can hang in the window letting everyone know that a member of this household is in the service. Mom has hers, but she is displaying two blue stars. If the star is gold, it indicates that their service member has been killed while in the service."

Jim glanced back at Anna and said, "Have you heard from Hazel as to what is going on with Daryl?"

Anna responded, "He left last Friday back to California, and Hazel said that Daryl was expecting to be heading over to Guam with his unit real soon."

At a far distance you could hear the clap of thunder and see the occasional streak of lightning, reminding you how hot the day was and that the heat that was moving upward was disturbed whatever was in the clouds passing by. It wasn't a storm coming, even though a storm might cool the evening down. It was heat lightning settling in for the evening before the night gave way to the darkness. Anna and Jim sat on that porch for several hours, content to be with each other, and even though they didn't enjoy the heat, they enjoyed the fact they were together, at least for now. The moon finally broke through the clouds as Jim glanced at the clock, seeing it was heading toward ten.

"I think it is time to move in," Jim said as he rose from his chair and reached for Anna's hand.

Jim went over and turned the box fan on that was in the bedroom window. Even though the air was still hot, it was better than nothing at all. Jim was finally in a real bed, not that plywood bed with a quarter inch mattress that the army had them sleep in. He looked at Anna and knew it was good to be home even if it was just for a little while. Jim lay quietly listening to the sound of the locust outside crying as if they too were protesting the heat. Their constant chirping soon had both Jim and Anna fast asleep.

It was almost seven when Jim arose, finding that somehow Anna had already dressed and gone to work. In the kitchen there was a note from Anna telling him she didn't want to wake him as he seemed a little restless and could use the sleep. The note went on to say that she had not sold the car, and if there was enough gas in the tank, he should go over and surprise his father. she should be home just after five. He placed the letter on the table and went over to the stove to find the coffee pot was only warm. So Jim opened the cupboard so he could make a fresh pot. Now Jim hadn't been around when the rationing started and didn't understand why there was very little of anything in the cupboards. There was probably enough coffee to make two more pots, and he was surprised to see how many boxes of macaroni and cheese she had on hand. He put the coffee back into the cupboard and decided to just reheat that which was already in the pot. Even warmed up coffee would be better than the field coffee the Army had them drinking.

Field coffee was coffee the cooks made by pouring pounds of coffee in a large tub of water. Once it came to a rolling boil, they would remove the pot from the fire and then dump eggshells from that day's breakfast into the pot which help settle the grounds to the bottom. After allowing the pot to sit for a few minutes it was ready to serve. Black, hot, and ready to enjoy?

Jim opened the refrigerator to find about six eggs, a stick of butter, and a can of opened peaches. There was a half bottle of milk and some fresh vegetables Anna had picked from the garden but very little of anything else. He closed the door and decided coffee was enough, at least for now. Just as he was heading for the porch, the phone rang. It was Anna.

"Jim, I only have a few minutes left in my break, but I imagine you have discovered not a lot in the cupboards and thought you might join me for lunch. I have an hour starting at eleven thirty."

Jim immediately answered, "Yes, I don't think I can do macaroni and cheese for lunch."

Jim and Anna enjoyed a good lunch of loose meat sandwiches and shared a slice of rhubarb pie from a small canteen that was located in an alley not far from where Anna worked. Anna explained the rationing process and how it worked so Jim would understand that even though he may have some dollars in his pocket, most items, except chicken, eggs, and dairy products, could only be obtained by a stamp.

"This rationing really makes planning a meal a little more difficult. But it is a system that allows for everyone to obtain the food they would need regardless of their financial status."

Anna explained that since she doesn't drive, she didn't have any gas stamps. So whatever was in the tank is all they would have until they could apply for a few gallons, or they can use public transportation. Jim understood that this war wasn't only going to be fought by the boys on the front line, but it was going to be waged by those who were on the home front too. He looked at Anna, gave her a kiss, and said, "I don't mind letting someone else drive."

Jim went over to his father's barbershop only to discover that it was closed, which seemed strange because Patrick never left the shop and even ate his lunch there between customers if needed. He started to go back to the car when he saw his dad rounding the corner carrying a small folder of papers.

"Jim," called out Patrick, "when did you get home, and why didn't you call?"

Jim explained that he got in yesterday afternoon, and it was a big surprise for Anna because he had beaten the letter home.

The two talked as Patrick tended to a few customers in the shop. Patrick told Jim that he had been at a training session learning about his responsibilities as the air raid monitor for his ward.

"Jim, I am not sure there is going to be much need for my services because I don't know how or why the Japs would want to bomb us. But with everything going on and all that everyone is doing, I figured it was the least I could be doing," he explained.

Jim said, "It seems everyone has made a commitment to this fight, so I don't see any chance in hell of either the Germans or Japanese winning this thing."

Patrick was looking at Jim, noting how handsome his boy looked in his uniform. The army had put some meat on his bones, and his shoulders appeared to be a little broader. "I see you don't need a haircut."

Jim snickered and said, "No, the army sees to it that my hair doesn't get too long."

"How long are you home for, son?" Patrick asked.

"I will be here until August 8, then I will be on my way to Abilene, Texas, to train in the field artillery on the 155mm howitzers."

"Do you know which way you're going after your training is done?" Patrick asked.

"No, at first I thought we were going to Camp McQuaid, California, and then to the Pacific, but my best guess now is Europe."

Patrick looked up. "Texas, I spent a month there one day," he said and then laughed.

Jim stood and said he had to go but agreed to bring Anna over for dinner at least one evening while he was back. He said he also wanted his dad to stop by the house before he had to leave so they could just talk.

As Patrick reached out and took Jim's hand, he said, "I tell you what, I will stop over the first of next week and bring a couple of cold ones if that works for you."

Jim nodded his head in agreement and headed to the door. Jim was cutting his visit short so he could go to the cemetery and stop by his mother's grave. Jim hadn't been to the cemetery to visit his mother's grave since they buried her in 1939 after she died from pneumonia. He recalled that she didn't suffer but that she had become so frail the last few years before she died. But Mom never complained, and even to her last day, she was there for him and his dad.

The county cemetery was just a short distance north of town, so it didn't take Jim long to get there. He parked the car and walked the short distance looking at each headstone until he finally came across a simple concrete headstone that read, "Margret B. McManis. Born August 2, 1898. Died March 31, 1939."

Next to her gravesite was his younger brother, George, who died at birth in 1923.

As he stood there quietly, his thoughts turned to her and the loving care she had provided his family for the short period she was here on earth. It seemed to be the same for all boys. No matter how big, how strong, or how old, they would always miss their mom; and at this point, Jim felt the emptiness of not having her here. He bent down, and with his handkerchief, he wiped the headstone clean, removing some dirt that had blown on it. Next to the grave was a small lilac bush that his dad had planted shortly after she had passed. He, like his father, knew how much his mother loved the smell of the blossoms each April, and now she could enjoy them every year for eternity.

Jim stood there just staring at the headstone, allowing thoughts of days long since passed to enter into his mind. He recalled so many events and moments realizing that life isn't about the time we spend here on earth, but it is about the times one shares with those we love that matter most. For that brief period, he felt his mom was with him. He somehow knew that she was telling him she was in a good place now and that he just needed to live his life with Anna and the family they someday would have together. After a brief prayer, Jim stood up, patted the headstone, and started his walk back to the car so he could pick up Anna from work.

* * * *

The time came for Craig and Art, who were both heading to the Great Lakes, to start their tour of duty in the navy. Craig didn't have to go through basic training, as he already did during World War I, but he did need to attend a school to learn the ways of the navy and to become a cook. He would be assigned to a Seabee outfit headed to Kodiak, Alaska, and Art, after his eight weeks of training, would get his wish to see that great big body of water by being assigned to a ship in the Pacific.

Mary stood quietly, waving her handkerchief as the train disappeared over the hill on its way to Chicago. She had done this before, but Anna could tell from the sadness in her eyes that experience didn't make saying goodbye any easier.

Mary looked to Jim and said, "Okay, take me home. I would like to get these darn shoes off and start super."

Anna and Jim enjoyed many evenings just being together. Jim even learned that public transportation wasn't so bad. He had discovered that if someone else was driving, he could be snuggling with Anna. They went skating; and even attended the dance at the local coliseum where they danced until one in the morning to Sammy Kay and his band, which had made a special trip all the way from New York.

They had a wonderful time regardless of the heat. Jim even tried his hand at the new dance called "the swing" but sat down when Anna suggested they try the jitterbug. Anna loved to dance, and she didn't even need to have a partner if the music got her to her feet. The evening finished with the hit song from Glenn Miller's band "Moonlight Cocktail." Anna and Jim danced around the floor as if they were skating on ice. They moved so effortlessly, not as a couple but as one like the rhythm of the music was guiding their feet. As the song ended, the light came up, and each couple made their way to the door. Jim and Anna could hear the distant sound of the last song playing as the band finished the last song of the set.

As Jim opened the door for Anna, she looked at him and said, "I love you, Jim."

As Jim started to close the door, he said, "That's good because I am going to be here loving you back for a very long time."

Jim's last Saturday evening with Anna was spent at the picture show. Anna had discovered that it was a place she could get away from the everyday grind and relax while being captivated by Hollywood. It didn't matter if it was an animated film like *Bambi*, a musical like *Holiday Inn* or *Yankee Doodle Dandy*, or if it was a comedy like *The Road to Morocco*. Anna enjoyed the time spent just being captivated and entertained. Tonight, however, she wanted to see *Casablanca* with Humphrey Bogart and Ingrid Bergman. A story of love, betrayal, and danger . . . where a nightclub owner helps an old girlfriend who was a part of the freedom fighters attempting to escape the Nazis. Where each kiss could be their last, and where love would be pushed to its limit.

The movie always started with a clip from the war, and tonight's clip was real footage from the Battle of Midway. The narrator described each event in detail, and with each Japanese plane hit or ship sunk, the room would explode in applause as it felt good to have something to cheer about. Jim went for popcorn during the cartoon and as he was taking his seat the feature presentation started.

With the credits running, Anna asked Jim for his hankie and noticed some redness around his eyes. She started to say something and then realized it wasn't necessary to ask something she already knew. Jim was a sensitive guy who understood the struggles and sacrifices of others, which was one of the attractions that drew her to him. She thought to herself, Men don't mind exposing their feelings as long as they don't have to talk about them, and she was okay with that. Jim gave her his hankie as he bent over to get his hat.

It was around nine when they walked out of the movie house to the trolley.

"Jim, do you want to go home now, or would you like to split a malt over at the Coffee Cup?" she asked.

The evening was still young, and the temperatures and humidity had seemed to take a break, so they not only decided to have that malt but walk home over the bridge and skip the ride.

Finally, the day came when it was time for Jim to pack his duffel bag and go back to the reality of his new life in the army. That morning, as Jim polished his shoes, Anna stood at the ironing board pressing all of Jim's uniforms, right down to his olive green boxer shorts. Jim was going to protest, telling her that it wasn't necessary when he realized it was something Anna wanted to do. So as she finished, Jim took each item and carefully folded and placed it in his bag.

Jim and Anna sat down to a supper of fried chicken, some handpicked vegetables from Anna's garden, and of course, macaroni and cheese, which had become a mainstay in most American family meals.

"Jim, what time do you need to be down at the train station tomorrow?" Anna asked.

"My train is scheduled to leave at 0845 hours, so I would imagine an hour before that should be fine. I need to show the agent my orders, and he is then supposed to hand me my ticket," Jim answered.

"If it is all right, can we take the trolley down to the station? I would like to sit with you while you wait?" Anna asked.

"It could be a while. You know how train schedules can be, especially in the morning," Jim responded.

Anna interrupted by saying, "Oh, I don't mind. I am off on Monday, so I really don't have anything else to do."

That evening, a terrible thunderstorm developed with bright lightning, loud claps of thunder, and pounding rain striking the window panes. It was raining and blowing so hard that Jim had to get up to remove the box fan and close the window to keep the rain from blowing into the bedroom. The noise from the storm would have kept anyone trying to sleep awake, but Jim and Anna didn't mind nor did they pay much attention, for this night was all about them and their last night together.

Anna sat quietly on the wooden bench inside the terminal holding Jim's hand as they talked and waited for the train. Soon, the first sound coming from the whistle could be heard, as the train entered the station. Jim looked up to the clock and said, "Wouldn't you know it? The damn thing is on time."

The porter announced the arrival and said, "Anyone departing to Saint Louis, Little Rock, Oklahoma City, and Dallas with a connection to Abilene, Texas, needs to board at this time."

Jim and Anna stood up and shared a long kiss as Jim pulled her close taking in the scent of her perfume. He wanted to remember how she felt, how she smelled, and how she looked so he could recall this moment every time he closed his eyes while he was gone.

Anna had decided she would not accompany Jim to the train. She had decided to stay behind; not wanting Jim to see the tears that she was sure would accompany his departure. She watched Jim as he walked through the doors and out to the train. He climbed the three steps and disappeared out of sight. Once he had boarded, Anna realized she couldn't stay behind, so she ran outside looking up to the windows trying to catch a glimpse of Jim for the last time.

He soon appeared at the window, lowering it so he could stick his head out, and yelled, "Here's looking at you, kid."

She laughed and blew him a kiss as the train started the slow grind of pushing it forward. The steel wheels struggled to grab the track, slipping and grinding until the struggle gave way and the train pulled away from the station. Anna stood on the platform watching as the train picked up speed and finally disappeared out of sight. The distant sound of the whistle was a reminder that once again she was all alone.

Jim stowed his gear, removed his hat, and settled in for the long ride. He looked out the window watching the Iowa countryside pass by, allowing each mile to settle in his memory as a reminder what he was fighting for and what he would be coming home to. He wasn't sure when that might be, but he took comfort in the belief that somehow he knew he would. He whispered out loud, "Next stop, Abilene."

Chapter 10

A HOME IN THE 678ᵀᴴ FIELD ARTILLERY

As Jim entered the depot, he couldn't believe how busy the train station was with it being so close to midnight. Everywhere he looked, he could see soldiers gathering their belongings and heading to waiting transportation to complete their trip.

Jim was looking for a sign indicating where he was supposed to go when a voice from behind him said, "Hey, private, you going to stay here, or do you want a ride to Camp Barkeley?"

Jim quickly turned to the voice and followed him out to a covered deuce and a half where several men were already on board. He handed his duffel bag up and climbed aboard.

As the trucks pulled away, Jim glanced out the back realizing the only thing he could see in the darkness were the headlights of a lot of other army trucks following theirs. There wasn't a lot of conversation as everyone was too tired to start any friendships. They would have plenty of time later to get to know each other. Jim glanced at the different shoulder patches and realized there were several MOS or military occupational skills, which must be training at this facility. They were signal, infantry, medical, armor, airborne, and of course, artillery.

"Want a smoke?" asked the corporal seated next to Jim.

Jim didn't smoke cigarettes often, but he was beginning to realize that there were times when having a pipe wasn't possible, and this was one of those times. The soldier was wearing a Red One shoulder patch, indicating he was a member of the first infantry division.

"Where are you from?" asked the corporal. "Ottumwa, Iowa," Jim said. "And you?" "Brooklyn, New York," he responded.

"The first is at Camp Barkley?" Jim asked.

"No, I am heading there to train some recruits and recover from some wounds I received while in Africa. I am hoping this assignment won't be long because I would really like to get back with my unit."

They finished their smoke without any further conversation and quickly fieldstripped the butt before throwing it out the back.

Upon their arrival, they were split into groups of fifty and led to temporary barracks where they could finally get some sleep. The bedding was already stacked on the bunks, so Jim leaned his duffel bag against the wall and made his rack as quickly as he could, not worrying about hospital corners or military correctness. All he wanted to do was climb in and get some sleep. Two days on the train had taken its toll, and Jim was looking forward to a few good hours of sleep without the noise from the train whistle or the bouncing of the tracks.

The next morning was like every morning since Jim entered the army. They woke before sunrise, dressed, and hurried outside where they stood in formation at attention, usually facing east, squinting as the sun broke. They stayed in that position while the flag was run up the pole and the national anthem played. As soon as the last note was played, a young second lieutenant informed them that they could do as they wished for the rest of the morning. He went on to say they needed to be in the assembly hall located by the main chapel by 1300 hours for a welcome briefing and orientation.

Jim took the opportunity after morning chow to look around the camp and get his bearings. He would learn that Camp Barkeley was becoming one of the nation's largest military camps for the war. It had been established in May of 1942 and was originally designed to be the home for the Medical Administrative Corps Officer Candidate School. The camp would grow to more than sixty thousand troops, making it twice as large as the city of Abilene, which was just eight miles outside the main gate. It had two thousand hospital beds, two cold storage plants, a bakery, four theaters, two service clubs for enlisted men, fifteen chapels, and thirty-five post exchange buildings. It was a city within the city that provided the troops with everything they would need, which was intentional to keep them out of the small towns and out of trouble.

Most of the men were housed in buildings called hutments instead of the barracks, which were used only for temporary assignments of the incoming troops. The huts were small buildings divided into rooms that housed about twelve to eighteen men. The living areas were cramped, and the buildings were so close together a soldier could easily pass something from the window of one hut through the window of another without leaving their rack. It was a practice that some of the soldiers used for profiting from the sale of candy, cigarettes, and magazines.

As Jim entered the assembly hall, he was taken aback to see more than three hundred men already in the room mulling around and talking. He wondered if all these men had arrived sometime yesterday like he did. Just as he moved down a row and found a seat, the command came bringing them all to silence and attention. They stood motionless as several senior officers and senior enlisted men walked on the stage.

"Take your seats, men. My name is Major General William S. Key. And I am the commander of the Forty-Fifth Infantry Division where most of you will be assigned. I want to welcome you to Camp Barkley. While you are here, you will be going through some of the most rigorous training you have had up to this point. Our purpose is to make sure you can carry out your mission, regardless of where you are, what the elements may be, and what is going on around you. You're going to train so much you will be able to do your job without thinking or without hesitation. When you think you have it down, we will do it again because we are going to be absolutely sure of your capability as a fighting unit. It is then we will be of service to this war and ultimately to its end."

After the general completed his remarks, the men were called back to attention as he left the stage. The rest of the briefing was delivered by a command sergeant major who covered logistics, expectations, and command. Once the command sergeant major was finished, the men were then broken out according to their MOS. Jim, now moving from coastal artillery to field artillery, got his assignment and where he was to report.

Jim made the two block walk over to the huts for the Seventh Corps, First Army division and asked a private where the orderly room was. He was directed down the hall, and as he looked in, he saw a sergeant sitting behind a typewriter slowly striking each key. He opened the door and approached the desk.

"Private McManis reporting as directed," Jim said.

The sergeant slowly turned around and looked at his paperwork. He then reached into a drawer and handed Jim new division shoulder patches and private first class stripes.

As he stood up, he said, "You're now a PFC, why, I couldn't tell you. You will have twenty-four hours to get the division patch and stripes sewed on all your uniforms, or you will be back to being a private. Now follow me." Jim followed the sergeant, who was a man of very few words, to hut eleven. They entered, and Jim saw seven men sitting on their bunks.

Each man was listening to another man they referred to as sticky Davis, relaying a story of some accommodation he received from some major for his snappy Manual of Arms.

The sergeant interrupted and introduced PFC McManis, telling them to get him situated and show him the living quarters. As Jim met the men who made up gun one of the 678th Field Artillery Battalion, Battery C, 155mm howitzer team, he heard a familiar voice coming out of the latrine. He turned to see Davidson approaching.

"Hey, Arky, what kept you?" Davidson asked as he stuck out his hand. "Well, I'll be damned," Jim said as he took Davidson's hand. "Now what are the possibilities that we would end up in the same outfit?"

Lad laughed and said, "I am not sure but figure the odds when you count that Merringer is also here."

They had no way of knowing, but the rest of the men who were assigned to the training platoon from Fort Wordon all went to Camp McQuaide, California, to continue at least for another year in the coastal artillery.

After Jim got settled and stored his gear, Lad suggested they head over to the day room where the battery had a few comfortable chairs, a pool table, a radio, and of course, coffee. The only way for the trainees to get around this large camp was either by jeep or foot, as none of them would be allowed permits to drive any personal vehicles. The men became so used to walking they referred to their boots as LPCs or leather personnel carriers because their boots spent so much time hauling their asses from one place to another.

Jim and Lad quickly changed into some comfortable civilian clothes before heading over. Jim asked if there was a tailor shop nearby so he could drop off his blouses to get the sewing done before the deadline.

Lad said it was on the way, so Jim got his uniforms, and they headed out the door.

Lad, who also had been promoted to PFC, looked at Jim and asked, "Jim, what are you going to do with the pay increase?"

Jim thought for a moment and said, "I hadn't given it much thought, but I would imagine I'll send most home to Anna and maybe pick up a few more dollars of life insurance."

The men could purchase, at a reduced rate, life insurance starting from one thousand to ten thousand dollars. The premium was based upon their age, and it was paid for through small payments taken from their pay. So Jim, who was now twenty-two, could buy life insurance at the rate of sixty-six cents per thousand.

The ground was damp from a brief morning rain, but with the light breeze, there was still a fine dust of the Texas soil blowing around. The sun was burning brightly and hot, and the only relief was the occasional cloud that blew by obscuring the sun if only for a brief moment. The humidity was at times unbearable, and to most, a new experience. Jim recalled what his father had said about spending a week in Texas one day and began to understand what he meant. No matter how new these elements were to the men, nothing was going to compare to the training they were about to go through. They were warned at the orientation, but there was no way to prepare for what lay before them or the amount of time they would be here.

The 155mm howitzer was an artillery piece that used comparatively small propellant charges to propel projectiles at relatively high trajectories with a steep angle of descent. Such weapons were characterized by a barrel length. The 155mm, referred to as "Long Tom," used separate loading ammunition and consisted of four components: a projectile, a bagged propellant charge, a fuse, and a primer. The propelling charge contained individual bags of powder which could be stacked or reduced to adjust for range of fire. It had a maximum range of fourteen miles and could maintain a rate of fire of forty rounds per hour.

Within the battalion, there were four batteries, each consisting of five guns. A single gun crew required ten men plus the driver. The weapon was towed by the M5 tractor, a fully tracked vehicle designed specifically to tow the 105 and 155mm howitzers. It carried the gun crew, their equipment, ammunition, and powder. It did not have any armor, so the only protection it had from enemy fire was the single mounted M2 Browning machine gun. The tractor was manufactured by International Harvester which, prior to the war, made construction equipment. The tractor was sixteen-feet long, weighed fourteen tons, and had a six-cylinder engine with a fuel capacity that could last for one hundred eighty miles before the need to refuel. What was unique about the M5 tractor was its rolling winch and roller system, allowing it to pull from either the front or rear.

Training was both intense and redundant with the days lasting over twelve hours. The men from Fort Worden, Washington, didn't seem to mind because they knew this training was going to serve them well for the action they were going to see in either the Pacific or European theater and not guarding the coastline, which was their original assignment. They would bivouac at least four of the seven nights a week so they could do nighttime fire missions. On one of these occasions, when none of the sergeants was around, Max, Stinky Davis, who hailed from La Crosse, Wisconsin, decided to pour five gallons of gasoline down the barrel to light up the night skies. Well, when the order to fire was given, a huge fireball erupted from the barrel. All the men who were unaware of their actions were startled at first, but realizing what had happened, they began to laugh.

Otto looked at Stinky immediately and said, "Damn, that looks like you when you use to sit on your bunk at night and light one of your farts."

The laughter didn't last long as First Sergeant Johnson appeared and started inquiring as to who was the wise guy that performed this trick. The first sergeant was a career soldier who was in the cavalry during World War I. His no-nonsense approach to soldering would mean extra duty for all the men, not to mention off-base passes canceled if they didn't give Stinky up.

One by one, the men told the first sergeant they were too busy with the fire mission to see who may have done that.

The first sergeant looked at each man. "I had better never see that again," he growled as he turned and walked away. The men didn't see the little smile on the first sergeant's face as he realized the men of the gun had just become a team.

With each training session, the men became better and more efficient at setting up the gun, completing a fire mission, hitting their target—which took a while—and then tearing it down and moving so they could do it all over again. The men would grow weary of the monotony of this routine, and the commander realized it was time to issue passes before the boredom started to show in their performance. Each member of the Battery C was issued weekend passes to go into Abilene.

It was Friday night, and after formation, the men changed into their "Class B" or dress uniforms consisting of an olive-drab (OD) wool garrison cap, OD wool trousers, and an OD wool shirt with a khaki cotton tie and russet brown Type I service shoes. They were reminded that even though they had passed for the weekend, they still had to be back on post by 2300 hours. In the final formation, the men received strict instructions about where they could go, how they were to behave, and more importantly, what they could say.

"Remember, what you say about your training here at Camp Barkley can and probably will kill a soldier," First Sergeant Johnson told them.

The men waited outside the main gate for a local bus to pull up to take them the few miles into town. As the men from Gun One boarded, they started talking about the dance at the USO club that night. Now, only Otto Merringer and Jim were married, so the other men were excited to meet the ladies from Abilene.

Stinky said, "If any of you guys want to score with a Southern belle, you had better hang out with me tonight."

From the back of the bus, an unidentified voice responded, "What did you have to eat for supper?"

Everyone laughed as Davidson said, "Oh, that is funny! Tonight, all I want is a few cold beers and maybe a chance to talk to anyone better looking than you guys."

Most of the men headed to the local bar for a cold beer or a shot of whiskey to get rid of that Texas dust that was always stuck in their throats. In this west Texas countryside, dust was always rising, falling, or blowing around. One eats it, breathes it, and wears it as if it were a part of their skin. You can't even avoid it after a rain shower. You could be standing with your feet buried in mud, and from somewhere, the wind will find dust and blow it your way to harass your eyes and nostrils.

Davis, Corporal Chick Heseltine, and PFC Kelly Brooks decided they would go straight to the USO club to secure a table, knowing there would be more men than tables soon enough. Now having Chick with them was a plus, as he was certainly a ladies' man. He stood six feet three with a very muscular build. He had broad shoulders, blond wavy hair, and dark blue eyes. His skin was dark from all the exposure he had to the California sun and the salt from the ocean. They called him "Hollywood" because he came from Los Angeles, and he looked like he should have been a movie star. Brooks was a plumber from Horseshoe Bend, Arkansas, who they nicknamed "plunger." Brooks was about five feet nine, and his waistline was about the same size as his chest. He had red hair with green eyes and that slow southern drawl that sometimes made it difficult to understand just what he was saying.

To the surprise of just about everyone, Davis was a very good dancer. He was on the floor doing the jitterbug, swing, or you name it. If they played a song, he could dance as if he had someone choreograph each step. It was Davis, and not Hollywood it seemed, that all the ladies wanted a shot on the dance floor, and Stinky was happy to comply. One had to wonder where a teacher from La Crosse, Wisconsin, would have learned to dance like that.

All the men, except Jim and Otto, took a turn or two on the dance floor. They seemed very content watching the others as they relaxed and enjoyed their free time and, of course, their common enjoyment for a good pipe. Otto talked about his civilian job of being a clown with the Barnum and Bailey Circus—the faces of the children and their laughter. But he also spoke of the loneliness of being on the road and away from his wife.

Otto said, "You know, Arky, I think after this war, I will have enough of being away from the wife, and it will be time to settle into one of those nine-to-five jobs."

Jim was relighting his pipe as he said, "I hear you. Being home every night definitely can have benefits."

The bus ride back to the base was relatively quiet with the occasional conversation being heard about either Davis's dancing or some gal the men had met. The desert area can get cold at night, so most of the windows were up with just a few cracked a little to allow the smoke to escape.

From the quiet and out of nowhere, a voice yelled, "Oh my god, Davis, put your damn window down."

Some things were never going to change.

* * * *

The days became weeks, and the weeks gave way to months as the 678th continued their training. They became proficient in uprooting a whole, carefully erected setup in a hurry, moving to another location on a map and firing. If they had ammunition, they fired it. No longer were they hiking mile after weary mile through choking dust draped with web equipment and small arms wearing their steel pots. The unit was now on wheels and tracks, and they made the most of it.

The men that made up Battery C worked day in, day out as each man learned the specialties of his specific task on the gun crew. They trained in the cool dampness of the morning under the blistering heat of the afternoon sun or in pitch blackness on those moonless nights. They performed each fire mission with precision and accuracy as they became an effective team capable of carrying out any fire mission under any condition without reservation.

When in the field, the men had to share their quarters with every creature that crawled or flew. Chiggers that lurked in the grass where they bivouacked or maybe the thousands of ants and grasshoppers who somehow found their way into the men's mess kits. On many occasions, the rattle of a nearby rattlesnake taking a nap near a mesquite tree reminded the men that he wasn't in any mood for their nonsense nor did he want to move.

Any free time the men got was spent writing letters, sleeping, or caring for their equipment. No long furloughs were issued, and passes were limited to a few hours so they could go to the base club, exchange, or an occasional movie. Speculation was no longer on if the battalion would go overseas but was about which ocean and when. Most every unit slated for overseas movement hoped it would be the Atlantic to fight against the Germans and not the Pacific to fight against the Japanese because the jungles and conditions would be at their worst for a field artillery unit.

Finally on September 2, 1943, almost one year from the date most of these men arrived at Camp Barkley, their movement orders came through. They were not told the theater of operation they would be going to, as the command felt it best they didn't know, at least until they were away from civilians who might want to know their movement orders. The men were upbeat because their training was finally over, but most of all because they would finally be getting the hell out of Texas.

Chapter 11

TIME TO CROSS THE BIG POND

Things were happening very fast as the battalion was preparing to move all their equipment to Camp Bowie, which was near Brownwood, Texas. Much to the complaints of the men, it appeared they were not done with their training in Texas, at least not yet. Camp Bowie was known as the overnight stop on their way to a Port of Embarkation. It was also where the battalion would be tested under realistic battlefield scenarios to see if they were ready for an overseas assignment.

The housing facilities and recreational opportunities at Camp Bowie were superior to those the men had at Camp Barkley. However, it really didn't matter as the time they spent in garrison would not be long. Within three days of their arrival, they were moved to the field where for the next three weeks, they would train, practice, and start the evaluation process.

The AGF or Army Ground Forces test was conducted during the last four days of their bivouac. The umpires evaluated every movement, looking at their abilities and capabilities. At the end of the third day, one day earlier than expected, the judges concluded that the members of the 678th Field Artillery Battalion had demonstrated professionalism and enthusiasm throughout the test, indicating a very high state of morale, proficiency, and readiness. The umpires saved some of their most flowing comments for the members of Gun 1, Battery C, who they said had demonstrated the highest level of readiness, morale, and teamwork they had ever seen in any fighting unit during any test conducted up to this point. The bottom line was what the men of the 678th had been waiting for; they were cleared for combat.

With promotion in hand and new stripes sewed on, the real work began for the unit and the men. The next phase was called POM or Preparation for Overseas Movement, another alphabetical arrangement that would mean tiresome lectures on shadeless parade fields or while seated in overcrowded auditoriums.

They were inspected in ranks and in their barracks. They were inspected as a group and often as individuals. Sometimes, they were inspected once a day, sometimes twice. They were well groomed, disciplined, and kept at a high level of readiness. They became proficient in such matters as map reading, chemical warfare, and military protocol. They would check in equipment, check out equipment, take medical examinations, and of course, get more shots.

During the morning hours, the men would work tirelessly getting their equipment packed or created so it could be transported by train to wherever they would be going. Track vehicles were driven up on flat cars and chained downed, while the howitzers were carefully lifted aboard, chained down, and covered with canvas to protect the weapon and to distort the exact item that someone may be looking at as it passed by. All the remaining equipment they would need was packed, marked for quick identity, and moved for shipment. The men were ready, even though they still did not know the destination of their train.

Afternoons were usually reserved for recreation or free time for the men. A time to do laundry, write letters, maybe catch a nap. But usually this time meant playing softball. They formed a league which would match one gun crew against another, and they would play until there was only one gun crew still standing on the field. They would be crowned the battalion champions, and each member of the championship crew would receive a seventy two hour pass.

Jim, Otto, and Stinky were seated on a jeep watching a game that Davidson and Brooks were umpiring when they noticed Captain Dallas approaching. Captain Joseph W. Dallas was the battery commander who held the men in his command to a very high standard. He believed how a soldier wore his uniform spoke volumes about himself, the unit he represented, and his ability to soldier. He believed in respect, discipline, esprit de corps, and tradition. He was a West Point graduate from the class of 1938, and he was a no-nonsense type of officer who cared for his men but understood the term "mission first, men always."

As he got closer, Jim and the rest of the men started to jump down from the jeep.

"Soldiers, where are your hats?" he asked. "I understand this may be a recreational period, but you're still wearing the army uniform, and I would expect any man from my battery to wear it correctly."

"Good afternoon, Captain," Jim responded as he reached in his pocket, pulled out his hat, and correctly seated it on his head.

"Afternoon, Sergeant. I hear Battery C no longer has any gun crews still in the competition."

"I guess we can shoot, but we can't hit," Stinky replied. "Sir, have you heard anything as to where we might be headed. I am really growing tired of the wait."

"No, I have not been informed as of yet. All I can tell you is don't wish your time here in the States away too quickly. I know you're anxious to get going, and so am I, but I can assure you once there, you will wish for days like this one."

The captain looked at his watch and said, "Carry on, soldiers." The men saluted as Captain Dallas, turned, and walked away.

As he walked away, Otto said, "We are lucky to have him. I know we can follow him anywhere because the outside may be West Point, but the inside is just another G.I. Joe like us who wants to do his job and then go home."

Jim spoke up and said; "I agree. He isn't looking for promotions, medals, or fame. He just wants to lead his men and do the job we are being sent to do."

The other men nodded their heads in agreement as their attention went back to the game.

* * * *

On November 4, 1943, the batteries of the 678th boarded the train for a three-day ride to Camp Kilmer located in New Jersey. There, they would go through the final stages of POM which would now include the briefing about what they could and could not write about from that time forward. They learned that their mail would be censored from this point forward, and anything thought to be too revealing would be marked out.

Jim wanted to write to Anna and let her know that he was heading overseas, even though he didn't know the exact location in Europe. So he simply wrote, "Anna, I am at Camp Kilmer, New Jersey. I cannot tell you where I am going as I do not know, and even if I did, the censors would remove it from this letter. I will not be able to write or contact you for a while. Please do not worry about me. I am fine, and the army is taking good care of me. I will send you an address where you can write as soon as I know. I miss you, and I love you. Jim."

After their arrival at Camp Kilmer, and once they were settled, passes were issued very liberally, allowing the men time to visit the cities in New Jersey or take in the sites of New York. Most of the passes were for twenty-four hours, and a few were issued for three days to those who had homes and family close by.

The entire Gun One crew headed into New York City. Jim walked around looking at the enormity of the city, its buildings, and its people. He had never seen so many people in one area as he was seeing now. Things were expensive, at least much more than he was used to paying back in Abilene. Many of the men wrote home asking for money, realizing this was the last fling they were going to have and maybe the last time they would be in such a place.

Jim, Otto, Lad, and a kid named Kelly Walsh from Flagstaff, Arizona, were satisfied with taking in the sites. They took the bus to the Empire State Building where they, like all visitors, took the ride to the top so they could look out on this incredible city.

Corporal Walsh said as he looked out, "I have been to the Grand Canyon on many occasions, and its beauty and splendor never cease to amaze me, but I have never seen a view like I am seeing now."

They walked completely around the observatory, taking in the panoramic view before grabbing the elevator and heading back down to grab a bus out to see the Statue of Liberty. While at Ellis Island, Jim was able to find the records of his six times great-grandfathers who arrived in 1757 from Ireland. This was the beginning of a dream for his family, and now he was being called to defend that dream. Getting a little tired from the sightseeing, the men decided to grab the bus and go down to the USO club.

The club was like a home away from home, where the coffee pot was always on, sandwiches made, a comfortable chair available, and there would be someone from the area to talk to or ask questions of.

Everywhere you looked, you saw men—sailors, marines, and other soldiers—walking around staining their neck as they looked up at the skyline. It was an unbelievable city, one that seemed to never stop nor sleep. Most of the men also postponed the need for sleep as they wanted to take in every possible moment before they were called to board a ship and leave all this behind.

Tomorrow was Thanksgiving, and the men of Gun One were all invited to a traditional Thanksgiving feast at a family's home in New Jersey who they had met through the USO. Of course, they thanked their host and accepted the invitation, realizing the meal she would be serving would be far superior to the one the army would be serving.

On Thanksgiving morning, the men learned that, unfortunately, they would not be showing up for dinner. It was on this day, November 23, 1943, that they received their orders moving them out of Kilmer and to the harbors in New York City to set sail on His Majesty's troop ship, the Carnarvon Castle, for England.

The men stood on the deck watching as the tugs slowly pushed the ship away from the harbor so they could start the departure out to sea. Most stood silently as they passed by Lady Liberty standing before them with her torch reaching to the sky. The realization was sinking in as they saw her slowly give way to the open water of the Atlantic.

Once at sea, the men sat down to an English version of a Thanksgiving meal. They would soon discover that the English had a unique manner where they could cook the flavor out of anything they touched, and each dish tasted just like the one they just had. If they found something which had some natural flavoring, they immediately cooked that flavor out of it.

Coffee wasn't any different it seemed. They knew as a rule Americans didn't care for tea, which was probably the only thing they could cook. So they made their version of coffee. It looked like coffee, but besides the resemblance, there wasn't anything else that would tell you what you were drinking.

"Damn army," Davidson said as he sat his fork down next to his plate. "With all the waiting we have done, you would have thought they could've let us have this one day to enjoy a good old American Thanksgiving meal."

Lad wasn't one to complain, but his thoughts and the conversation switched to the family who had prepared a meal that no one was going to come to and they had no way of knowing why.

"I bet that lady could cook," said Hollywood.

"I can almost taste the stuffing and see the crispness of that big bird she was going to serve us, that is until I put this crap in my mouth," said Otto.

As the men were finishing their dinner, First Sergeant Johnson came by the table to inform them they would have the first watch of manning the ship's guns. During the twelve-day voyage, each battery would take six-hour shifts behind the guns mounted around the ship. Their duty was to keep a sharp lookout for enemy submarines and be prepared to fire on them when ordered. The Germans had learned, from past voyages, the lanes the ships would be taking and had, in the past, launched several successful attacks, sending many of them to the bottom of the Atlantic.

When the men weren't standing a watch, cleaning equipment, or doing calisthenics up on the deck, they used their spare time writing letters to mail once they landed. Many tried to get the sleep they had lost while in New York, and many played cards. Payday craps was the game of choice. They would stand in long lines at the ship's exchange counters, stocking up on candy, cigarettes, tobacco, matches, chewing gum, and stationery.

It was cold, and the seas were rough. With so many men being sick, it was hard to tell if the men were reacting to the constant movement of the ship or from the food they were trying to digest. Down at the mess, one had to forget his manners and keep an arm up on the table so his tray wouldn't slide off or down the table. On more than one occasion, someone would walk away, and the next sound you would hear was a metal tray clanging to the floor, throwing his dinner all over everything or everyone.

On this voyage, each soldier was given two books for information they would need to read prior to landing. The first was a prayer book for soldiers and sailors. It contained prayers, hymns, and verses from the Bible that the service member could use during church services that were held each morning after exercise. The second was a book informing them of how they were to behave once they landed in England.

The book tried to address any resentment for the British the American soldiers might have by drawing comparisons to themselves, with language, democracies, and freedoms of speech, religion, and sports. The differences highlighted were that the British people are more reserved and preferred tea, which wasn't hard to understand after one tried their coffee. A reminder was emphasized not to brag about bailing the Brits out during World War I. In that war, the American losses were around sixty thousand men compared to the one million that the British people lost. They served their beer at room temperature, drove on the left side of the road and from the right side of the car. The American soldiers made considerably more money than their British counterparts who were also fighting this war.

London was not just in the war, but their city was a war zone. Every light, including the street lamps, was blacked out to protect against German air raids. All the factories were producing products used for war, which meant an incredible shortage of things like gas, clothing, soap, food, furniture, and so on. The fields were used to grow wheat and the flower gardens were producing vegetables to help feed an army. Britain looked hard and tattered, not at all what the British people wanted to leave for your first impression. The British people were proud people determined to crush Hitler, and they welcomed the help from America.

* * * *

On the fifth day of the trip, the men were awakened by the sound of general quarters. It appeared that a German U2 boat was spotted, and two U.S. destroyers were quickly summoned to come alongside and start the process of dropping depth charges trying to either force it to service or sink her. As the danger subsided and the destroyers sailed away, it became apparent the sighting may have only been an overzealous sailor who thought he saw a periscope in the water.

The men didn't mind the interruption, as they knew it was far better to be called to general quarters by someone who thought they saw something instead of not being called and taking a hit from a German torpedo. The emergency ended with no shots fired, no ship hit, and the only things disturbed were probably a few fish and a hot poker game or two. The men went back to their boredom of another day at sea as they continued the slow process to a location no one yet knew.

On the seventh day at sea, the men were informed that they would be arriving at Southampton. From there, they would travel by train to the town of Swanage in Dorset, England. Before the war, Swanage was a popular resort town where the English people came to relax, enjoy the countryside, and of course, take advantage of the small shops and pubs—something the American soldiers would also take advantage of once they were there.

It was on December 4, 1943, that the men of the 678th Field Artillery stepped onto foreign soil. They immediately saw the results from the war because the city had recently been bombed. The raids destroyed several buildings and businesses and killed sixteen of the town's citizens. You couldn't tell by the activity on and around the dock that the

German air raids had little if any effect on those who survived as they went about their business of day-to-day living.

The men were billeted in houses along the hillside that overlooked the bay and village. The climate was damp cold, and the only heat they had in their rooms was from a tiny wood-burning fireplace. After company C was settled, the men were released to trade their dollars in for pounds and pence and descended into town, which was less than a mile away. Jim, along with Lad, Otto, Max, and Chick, headed in just to walk around and get rid of their sea legs, which one gets after a few days walking around on a rolling ship.

The village was crowded as the men enjoyed the tea houses, pubs, cinema house, and dancehalls. Many of the men went about their business by downing many pale English bitters, ale, and what could be found of spirits. They sipped on some of England's finest teas while eating chips, sausage, sandwiches, and microscopic salads. The beer was room temperature as described in the pamphlet they had just read, but they discovered it wasn't that bad since the temperature of the room was usually in the fifties.

Everywhere the men went, there was a constant reminder that they needed to be on their best behavior as the military police patrolled the area. You did not want to be caught sleeping at a pub, in an alley way with a young lady or fighting with the civilian population unless you wanted to spend a few days in the stockade.

Southampton was a rough town probably because of the frustration the people who lived there felt from the bombing and the helplessness they had of not being able to do much about it. You didn't have to look for trouble; it would find you, as the members of Gun One would soon find out. English sailors and soldiers took exception to the Americans, which often led to fisticuffs. It wasn't over international affairs, but most often, they felt the Americans were too brazen and too forward, especially with the British ladies.

Davis and Chick were on the dance floor impressing the ladies when a few British soldiers came out on the floor, cut in, and tried to move them off the floor.

Hollywood took exception and stepped back in saying, "Why don't you sit down and drink your ale? You can have the next dance, if the ladies agree."

Those comments were met by a fist that came out of nowhere striking Chick across his nose, breaking it. Davis went flying over and on the table knocking it and the drinks that were on it, all over the men sitting at the table. Jim, Davidson, and Brooks were all on their feet. A few fists were thrown before all the men scattered when they heard the distant sound of the MP whistle. None of the men was going to hang around to explain who was at fault because they knew that would result in them spending the evening in the brig and then trying to explain their behavior to First Sergeant Johnson. The marks on their faces and the cuts on their hands were going to be difficult enough to explain.

On March 28, the battalion received orders moving them to a place called Twenty Grand. This was a tent city miles away from any cities and away from the British soldiers and citizens. It was decided it was best for all parties if they moved away from the city and away from any distractions that might affect the men's readiness and focus. They were confined to this area to pull maneuvers and fine-tune their skills until spring. As the spring rains were beginning, the 678th received new movement orders sending them to the coastline to join the First Army under the command of General Omar Bradley who would oversee the American landings on Omaha and Utah Beaches.

General George Patton and his Third Army were still in the United States. Information was purposely leaked to the Germans who were convinced that Patton was in command of the First United States Army Group and was planning the invasion of France by attacking Pas de Calais. To feed the Germans' beliefs, the Allies created an invasion force with fake tanks, artillery, and landing craft. They made sure the Germans could see the force, which was placed along the shoreline near Dover, England, a location that was across the channel from Pas de Calais just one hundred and fifty miles away. The use of life-sized rubber blowups of actual military equipment would convince any spy that this was indeed an actual invasion force requiring the Germans to react for the attack by sending their troops and equipment to Calais and away from where the actual invasion would take place. Normandy.

Chapter 12

D-DAY AND BEYOND

For the last four days, the rain continuously pounded the coastline. The seas were so rough that the ships in the harbor were being tossed around as if they were at sea, and the men aboard became ill. The readiness of the invasion force was growing weary as day in, day out the weather report was the same.

Davidson entered the tent and remarked, "I don't remember the last time I saw the sun. I mean, I know it's daytime, but when I look in the sky, all I see are gray clouds and gloomy weather."

Everyone was tired of being cooped up, and if you went anywhere, you had to track your way through the slush and mud that bogged down the men and their spirits. The tents had become so saturated from the rain that if you touched the canvas, rain started leaking where you just made contact. Tempers were tested as men became on edge and little things that would normally not even draw a reaction now drew a growl or an occasional fist. The command knew this weather was taking its toll and hoped they would get a break soon.

Jim was sitting on his bunk listening to the rain and reading a new book the army had passed out called France—a thirty-six-page pamphlet which every soldier was given prior to D-Day. The men were informed that they could expect a huge welcome from the French people, and they were not to look down on their failure in the war thus far. It told of the sacrifice they were making. It stated that on an average day, a Frenchman would be shot every two hours. Their underground created many obstacles to the Nazi Army, which took their attention away from the invasion and toward those activities. It went on to say that the French were very proud people, and most of them were living off the land they called home. Germany had stolen anything and everything and sent it back to their homeland. They took any food and wine they could find and used it to feed their army, leaving the French with nothing. Many of the French people had died from hunger, and the GIs were cautioned to only eat the rations they were provided. They were told not to take what little food the French people had even if food was offered. The pamphlet encouraged them to share any food they did not want with the French people, especially their canned fruit and chocolate, as that may be all they would have to eat that day.

Again, they were warned not to get friendly with any of the local prostitutes and not to trust the health card they may carry. Most of these ladies were probably Nazi undercover agents who were trained to get information from a talkative soldier who would be willing to trade information for a few minutes of pleasure. The guide told of a war-ravaged land that had been stripped bare by the conquering army. The pamphlet concluded with the urgency and need to liberate France. It was the soldiers' duty to return this land, despite the odds, back to its citizens and rid them of the German Army.

Finally, the weather broke, and on June 6, 1944, D-day was launched, releasing the largest amphibious landing in the history of war. Over one hundred and fifty thousand American soldiers would assault the beaches of Omaha and Utah. And thousands of Allied paratroopers would jump behind enemy lines at night, securing key roads and bridges.

As the sun rose on Normandy, the Allies began their amphibious landings. The men climbed down rope ladders and into small landing crafts that were lowered from the decks of larger ships to make their way onto the beaches. The assaults on the beaches were going as planned. The only exception was at Omaha Beach where the U.S. First Infantry Division was involved with one of the fiercest battles of the war. Surrounded at both ends by cliffs that rose like giant walls from the sea, they had to fight for every inch of sand they would claim as they came ashore. Many didn't even get out of their landing craft, as they were gunned down by heavy machine gunfire as soon as the landing craft door opened. Many drowned as they jumped over the side trying to avoid being hit by the wall of bullets entering the craft. They discovered that the depth of the water, along with the equipment they had on, pulled them down to the floor of their make-shift grave. The Germans had a fortress atop the cliffs overlooking Omaha Beach from the west. Those who were lucky enough to get out of the landing craft had to cross more than three hundred yards of beach filled with man-made obstacles and under intense fire. As a result, soldiers ran onto the beach in groups and became easy targets. This day would account for over nine thousand Allied killed, and more than one third of these fell at Omaha Beach.

The plan called for the invasion force to advance five to ten miles after twenty-four hours of fighting. But with the stiff German resistance, the invaders were held up on the beach, making the progress inland excruciatingly slow and painful. It would take the Allied forces two days to reach the day-one goal. But taking control of the beaches and moving inland opened the beaches now for the support unit and replacements to come ashore.

The 678th Field Artillery came ashore on D-Day plus three as an attachment to the First Army. Their mission was to provide additional artillery support for the ground troops who just days before had paid the high price for this newly obtained real estate they were on. As the men of Battery C came ashore, they saw the devastation from the fight that had taken place. As men and equipment rolled in, the members of grave registration were working continuously trying to identify, notify, and bury the dead. On the top of the cliffs, they could hear the sounds of large bulldozers busily digging long trenches so those men could be buried in their final resting place. Compared to a few days ago, this was now a very peaceful place that overlooked the beaches as the surf softly pounded the shore; a place that matched two armies in an intense struggle both determined to stand and succeed; a place where, despite the odds for survival, the men who made up the Allied forces pushed forward because going back wasn't an option. But for too many men, it was the final place they would see on this earth.

Jim, like all of the men from Gun One, said nothing as they moved their equipment forward. What was there to be said? No words could express what they felt nor describe what they saw. Everywhere they looked was the evidence of the hell the initial waves endured to claim the space they now stood on. Landing craft still smoldering, holes blown deep in the sand, steel entrapments bent and tossed around like pick-up sticks from a kid's toy box, and fires glowing from burnt out bunkers. There was individual equipment drifting into the shore line with each wave, slowly making its way from a soldier who never felt the sand beneath his feet. All of what they saw only added to their resolve to see this fight to end and to free a world from the terror of a madman. As they passed by this reminder of what war would be like, they felt no fear because fear keeps your feet from moving forward. With youth, there is a belief that no matter what you see, it won't happen to you, regardless of the evidence that makes the argument to the contrary.

They pushed north, heading to catch up with an advancing army who was facing a German Army that had a heavy presence and had shown no signs of running. The Germans knew this day would come, and the months of preparation would be to their advantage, while the Allies slowly made their advance over grounds filled with minefields and obstacles designed to slow them down or draw them into a fight.

The weather had improved, and the cloud cover, along with the coolness of the breeze coming inland from the channel, provided some comfort for their work. There were spots that slowed them down as they passed through plowed fields and muddy roads that bogged down the heavy guns. The battalion paused and made bivouac at Le Havre, France. It was located on the mouth of the river Seine on the English Channel. The Germans, who had occupied the city, were devastated during the recent battle that killed over five thousand people and destroyed twelve thousand homes, mainly by Allied air attacks. Now the city was a stop-off place as men and supplies came ashore. The headquarters battery continued forward to meet up with the command element, review maps, and get briefed on the orders they would be carrying out the next few days.

The remaining batteries went about their business of attending to their equipment and drawing ammunition and the supplies they would need. There were no buildings fit for housing the men or the guns, so they attended to their personal needs by finding a place to roll out their bedroll and get some hot coffee made.

Jim and Lad were sitting next to a track vehicle, enjoying a pipe, when Captain Dallas approached the men at the gun.

"Corporal, have you seen Lieutenant Farr?"

Corporal Anthony piped out, "Sir, I haven't seen that son of a bitch all day, sir."

The captain took a long look at the corporal and the rest of the men who were shaking their heads in agreement and walked away. Now the lieutenant had just passed through the area checking on the guns about twenty minutes before, but Anthony, like most of the men, didn't care for the lieutenant and had decided to tell a small fib. He figured the captain would rip him a new asshole when he found him because he believed an officer first attended to the needs of his men before he attended to his own.

Second Lieutenant Charles Farr, a ninety-day wonder from some Ivy League school, received his commission because of his father's position and not because of his military knowledge. The men didn't care for him because he didn't really care for them. He knew he was better than the enlisted men, and he saw each soldier as a pawn he could move around like in a game of chess to gain some kind of advantage now so he could have a political future when the war ended. Corporal Jack Anthony, nicknamed "Yankee" because he hailed from Adams, Massachusetts, didn't care for the lieutenant for all the same reasons but especially because Farr was from Texas. Anthony really didn't care for anything or anyone from Texas, and the time he spent in Abilene only compounded his dislike.

The next morning, after a cold breakfast, the batteries continued their movement north to join up with the headquarter's battery who had established their position to support the division. Each division had the support of four field artillery battalions. The battalion HQ was equipped with three batteries, each possessing four 155mm howitzers. It was the mission of the 678th to destroy anything that could aid or support the enemy, to move the Germans in a direction toward a place that the Allied troops would be waiting, and to destroy or slow down anything that would allow the Germans to escape.

The Germans had been in France since May of 1940, and moving them out was going to be a very long and difficult task. In June of 1940, the French cabinet signed a cease-fire, thus ending the hostilities and surrendering the North and West regions to the Germany Army. France had agreed to be subordinate to the invading force, and the remaining third of the country was set aside as a liberated zone under the control of Vichy headed by Maréchal Philippe Pétain.

The entire coastline was declared a military zone, thus making it off-limits to any French civilians, except those local inhabitants who were required to carry a special pass. Many of the families who lived in that area took refuge by moving inland to Vichy, considered a safe zone. It was obvious why the Germans wanted the coastline, but just as important was to control the agriculture which would not only feed the army but could be easily transported back to the motherland.

* * * *

The 678th arrived on site around noon and moved their guns into position overlooking the small village of Littleville. The men of Battery C wasted no time in getting their guns set up. Davidson went forward to set up the aiming stakes, which were used to traverse the gun to a fixed target. Jim, Stinky, Otto, and Hollywood started the process of unloading crates that house the projectiles they would be using on the assault and the charges that were individually packed in their metal canisters. The remainder of the crew stockpiled the powder in a place to keep it dry from the evening's air and from any rain that was still possible.

After the men had readied their position, they turned their attention to preparing for the evening. While most paused for a smoke, Otto started digging a foxhole. When asked what he was doing, he said, "I am digging a foxhole, so in case we get attacked, I am going to have something to jump into."

This would become routine for Otto. Every time the battery stopped, regardless of the amount of time, Otto got out his shovel and dug, thus earning him the nickname of "Gopher."

As Otto was putting the finishing touches on his foxhole, Second Lieutenant Farr, and Lieutenant Mitchell, the battery forward observer, came by to inform them of an upcoming fire mission. Lieutenant Mitchell would position himself ahead of the unit located in the apple orchard overlooking the village. From there, he could see the targets and adjust the fire, so they would get the maximum effect of the guns. The lieutenant's job was very dangerous because once the attack started, the enemy would dispatch patrols looking for him. He had to be close enough to the target to call in the rounds and yet be alert for those who were seeking to kill him.

After the lieutenants left, Cookie and Plunger came up with an idea. While they were running the wire out to the observer's position, they would raid the orchard so they would have some fresh fruit to eat after the attack.

Cookie, whose real name was Billy Ray Barr, and who was a short order cook in a local hash house in Georgia before the draft board found him, said, "Maybe we can pick enough to get the battalion cooks to make us a pie."

From the rear of their positions, the men could hear sounds of the First Infantry Division that was passing by heading to a position where they would hold out until the shelling stopped. From that position, they would launch the assault on the village, driving any Germans out by going from building to building.

As Plunger watched out, he stood up and yelled, "Good luck!"

A young private looked back and said, "Blow them to hell for us."

"You got it, kid. They will be running before you get there," Hollywood answered.

As the sun was setting, the men anxiously prepared for their first fire mission. They had fired hundreds of rounds before, but this time, they mattered. They saw the faces of the men who were going forward and knew this time it was not only counted, but it mattered as in life or death.

Jim was finishing his last pipe when First Sergeant Johnson came up and said, "Okay, men, let's tear it down. We got new orders, and we need to be on the road in less than an hour."

Lad reached out to the first sergeant, grabbing his arm.

As he turned around, Davidson said, "Top, what about those men sitting out there in the tree line waiting for us to fire?"

Johnson looked in that direction, paused, and then said, "I don't know, Sergeant, but I am sure someone is moving in to take our place. Now you have your orders. Let's move and get these guns ready to roll."

The moon had broken over the clouds, allowing the convoy to move at a little faster pace than they would normally run on blackout. Blackout was running the vehicles with no lights, and the only thing the driver had to follow was the very small reflector on the guns. The men sat quietly on the M5 listening for any sound of another artillery unit taking on their mission. None came, or at least they never heard anything.

Arky felt a knot in his stomach as he thought about those boys who were preparing for the morning attack. "I can't imagine what is going through their mind," he said.

"I know," said Lad, "they are probably cursing us out, wondering where in the hell we went?"

Plunger spoke up, saying, "Maybe they will postpone the attack until they can get them some support."

"You're probably right," Jim said, trying to reassure the members of the gun crew as well himself, even though everyone knew that wasn't how the army operated. The army would go through with what they had to do.

The only sounds that could be heard were the sounds of the tracks as they made their way to a destination unknown. It wasn't long before, in the distance, they heard small arm fire with an occasional mortar round exploding. It was apparent the Germans were trying to push through a British unit that was barely hanging on and to make it to a bridge that would allow them to escape back into Belgium.

Jim jumped down from the halftrack as it backed the gun into position. The crew quickly went to work by spreading the legs of the gun and securing it to help prevent too much movement from the kickback once it was fired. An adrenalin rush kicked in wiping away and tiredness the men had felt up to now. Each man knew his job, and in no time Jim picked up the radio and said, "Gun One up and ready."

Ranger and Yankee were the two biggest men on the gun, and they could be seen tossing around those ninety-five-pound projectiles as if they were just horseshoes. Chick and Davis went about the business of removing the ring from the nose so Davidson and Otto could put the fuse in and the primer in the breech of the gun. Bobby and Kelly would be responsible for cutting and combining the correct amount of powder to send the projectile to its target.

Soon, a voice came over the radio giving the elevation and distance and telling them to arm each projectile with "HE" or high explosives. Once the type of round was known, Jim reviewed precalculated trajectory tables specific to that type of round. He set the elevation angle and the deflection that would guide the round to its target.

Once ready, the command came in. "Gun One fire, Gun Two fire."

And so it went until each gun had fired its first round. With each firing, the observer made adjustments until they were on their target. Once the observer was satisfied that each gun was on target, he commanded, "Fire for effect."

All four guns opened up, firing round after round, adjusting the gun after each shot until the order came in cease-fire—target destroyed.

They ceased fire and immediately went to policing the spent brass shells and attending to the position of the gun and their area. Finally, they received the order to stand down.

Nothing more came from the observer, and then they heard Captain Dallas say, "Good job, men, mission complete. Police your area and get some rest."

Jim felt a real sense of accomplishment knowing they had made a difference tonight. But no matter how much he thought about what they did here, he couldn't help but think of the mission they abandoned.

The next morning, the battery received orders to move forward. They had only proceeded a few miles up the road when they came upon a village. It didn't take long for the men to realize that while they were taking out the bridge, another unit was leveling every building in the town. It was a slow process as they tried to maneuver their way through the cluttered streets. The smell of buildings burning and gunpowder filled their nostrils as they looked around at the shells that once were shops, churches, schools, and homes. You could hear small explosions as the equipment the Germans had left behind was being destroyed. It was apparent, by the lack of bodies found, that the Germans had withdrawn quickly, deciding to fight another day at another place.

The batteries had to pause and wait for the combat engineers to bulldoze roads open so they could get their equipment through the rubble. While they paused, Sticky Davis and Cookie discovered a small wine shop in the only building not totally destroyed. The two men grabbed as many bottles as they could carry and headed back to the crew to share their treasure.

As the men sat waiting, somehow each of the bottles got opened; and before long, most of what was confiscated had been consumed.

Captain Dallas came by seeing the evidence of their find and said, "Men, I don't mind if you have a little wine now and then, but I would recommend you learn to put the cork back in it and save some for another day. Now I think you should take advantage of this pause and attend to yourself as it appears most of you could use a shave."

It wasn't until later in the afternoon they started toward their next destination. As they reached the outskirts of town, they saw a bridge that lay in the riverbed with the medals of the expansions blown all over the place. They also saw two German half tracks and one troop carrier along with several bodies lying lifeless next to the road and in the water. The men understood, and without saying a word, they knew they were looking at the results of their mission from last evening. Apparently, the Germans had decided to abandon the village and were attempting to cross when the fire mission started. There was no way of knowing how many troops escaped over this bridge, if any, but they knew these Germans didn't.

As the M5 track vehicle slowly made its way, Jim examined the damage. He, like all the men, were so tired from being awake for the last thirty-six hours that he felt nothing as a result of what he saw. He did not feel glee, sadness, or joy. He just examined the results of their work and looked out toward the horizon, wondering what this day would bring.

Staff Sergeant Donald (Arky) Vaughn

Chapter 13

WAITING ON THE NEWS

Anna came out to the kitchen to get herself a cup of coffee before she had to start getting ready for work. Before she sat down, she turned the radio on hoping to catch the latest news from the war. As she turned the dial, she couldn't help but think of all the times she had scolded Jim for doing the same thing when he first got up.

It was Tuesday, June 6, 1944; and to Anna's surprise, the airways were filled with information from both New York and London about the invasion that was taking place in France. As she was listening, the announcer broke away from the normal broadcast to the Supreme Headquarters of the Allied Expeditionary Force. It was a brief statement confirming that, under the command of General Dwight Eisenhower, Allied naval forces, supported by strong air support, had begun landing troops on the northern coastline of France. Major Eliot, a war correspondent, went on to describe the various phases of an amphibious landing operation and the difficulty of the effort.

The station went back and forth from their studios in New York to the war correspondents who were reporting from the ships that launched the invading force. They described the complete and utter surprise the invasion was to the Germans, who expected the attack to come at Pas de Calais.

Anna didn't want to move away from the radio as the information was coming in fast on the progress of the invasion. She realized with this news they would be really busy, so she got up from the table and headed back into the bedroom to finish getting ready for work. She continued to listen when she paused, looked into the mirror, and said, "It has begun."

The moment a nation and a world had been anticipating. The inevitable start they all knew had to come to rid the world of the Nazi stronghold on Europe and the end of its terror. Anna felt joy, fear, and uncertainty as she listened to each detail as it was being reported.

The phone rang just as she was headed out the door, and she almost didn't answer, not wanting to be late for work.

But she picked up the phone to hear her mother say, "Anna, have you been listening to the radio?"

"Yes, Mom, I just shut it off. I am heading in to work." "Do you think Jim is there?" Mary asked Anna.

"No," Anna replied. "From everything I have been able to get from Jim's letters and description on the types of units that would be conducting this invasion, I don't think his unit is involved, at least not yet."

Anna wasn't sure if those words were meant to comfort her mother, or maybe they were directed for her self-assurance.

"May God be with each soldier today," Mary said as she hung up, knowing Anna had to go.

It was a very long and difficult day as the switchboard was lit up with calls. It seemed everyone in the community was calling trying to get information, talk about the events, or just send their thoughts to someone's family who might have a serviceman involved.

Even though it was against company policy to have any distraction in their area, the operators had a small radio on in the room so they could listen to the accounts from the attack. Anna couldn't help but eavesdrop, trying to listen for any news on what may be happening. All day long, as soon as Anna unplugged one conversion, another would come through. She patched each call swiftly as if she was in some kind of race, knowing at least to the person placing the call, it was urgent. Five o'clock came quickly as she ended her shift and unplugged her headset, allowing her replacement to take over.

Once she and Hazel were outside, they were caught off guard to see just how many people were just standing around on the street reading a paper or talking. Anna didn't often read the paper, but today, she would make an exception because she knew, from the bits and pieces of conversations she had heard, there was a lot of news to catch up on.

She headed over to where a young lad was standing on a wooden crate, holding up the afternoon's paper he had for sale with the single word headline that read "INVASION!"

She handed the boy a nickel, took her paper, folded it under her arm, and crossed the street to catch the trolley for the ride home.

The paper gave a very detailed timeline of what had transpired on this day. It started from the beginning with Germany's international shortwave service, Trans-Ocean, reporting that "a grand scale amphibious landing" was taking place along the northern coast of France near the Normandy Peninsula. It went on to report that the invading forces had pushed their way nine and a half miles inland near the city of Caen where they were digging in for the evening. She went on to read that the initial reports of casualties were less than anticipated with such a large-scale invasion. That was four o'clock in the afternoon

Central time, the last entry before they stopped reporting and went to print to meet the paper's deadline.

Anna folded the paper again and set it next to her. This paper needed to go in Jim's scrapbook or at least the front page needed to go in. She was glad to read the part about the casualties but wondered how bad they were. She thought for a wife or mother whose husband or son died today that they would think the cost was more than enough.

Anna arrived home to discover her mother was in her kitchen cooking and listening to the radio.

"Mom, what are you doing?" Anna asked.

"Oh, I couldn't sit in that house all alone any longer. I hope you don't mind? I thought you probably had a rough day, so why don't you change, and I will finish dinner for us?"

At first, Anna was a little put out, as she was looking forward to a quiet evening sitting in a hot bath while listening to some music from the radio and writing a long letter to Jim. As she changed, her mood changed knowing that her mother was just like everyone else on this day. She wanted to be with someone and not alone because this truly was the start of the worst this war was going to offer now that the Allied forces had stepped onto French soil.

She reminded herself that her mom had both a husband and a son in this and needed a little time with her only family member still at home, so she said, "Thanks, Mom. What are we having?"

After dinner, Mary sat in the big chair by the lamp and pulled out a scarf she had started.

"Mom, who are you making the scarf for?" Anna asked.

"Well, I am going to make two. This one I will send to your father in Alaska, and the other will be a dark green for Jim. I don't know what the military provides in the way of winter clothing, but I figured he could use a scarf this winter."

Anna agreed as she opened the drawer on the hutch and pulled out stationery and pen to write a letter.

"Mom, I am going to write Jim a letter if you don't mind. Would you like to listen to the radio?"

"As long as it isn't about the war, dear. I think I have had enough for today," she replied.

Anna turned on the radio and found the *Bob Hope* show. This was a very entertaining show that provided comedy skits and music from some of the top entertainers on the radio.

"How's this?" Anna asked.

"Great," answered Mary, "I just need some background noise to keep my mind on my work."

The next morning, Anna rose early and headed out to her garden. She wasn't scheduled for work, and although she needed to take advantage of the time, she had to do some work in the garden before the morning coolness gave way to the breaking sun.

Anna shared her garden with Hazel and a few of the ladies in the neighborhood. Each lady was given a few rows so they could plant some vegetables in hopes it would produce enough for them not only to enjoy this summer but enough to can and store for the winter. Everything they were able to grow would allow them to use the forty-eight points they received each month to buy other items, such as canned, dried, and frozen foods or so they could purchase other food like beef, pork, or butter. To have some meat in the house, other than chicken, was a welcome relief from the supplement they were growing tired of—macaroni and cheese or cottage cheese that was meant as a replacement for meat on their dinner tables.

As Anna was attending to the corn, she remembered Jim saying, "The corn should be knee high by the Fourth of July."

Anna looked at the crop and realized it already passed that old wives' tale a few days ago. She laughed because again, she didn't put much stock in these tales. Anna knew what really mattered was when you planted the seed, the type of soil you had, and how much rain and sunshine it got. With crops growing, her attention was on how she could keep the critters like rabbits and blackbirds from robbing her harvest.

Anna had turned the entire backyard—a little less than a quarter of an acre—into a garden. The food grown would be divided among the six families who were participating. They had planted beans, peas, asparagus, corn, and cauliflower. Hazel was trying her hand at watermelon and pumpkins.

If it wasn't for rationing, life in this small community wasn't too bad. There was plenty of work, and for those who were so inclined, there was plenty of overtime work available. John Deere had switched from producing farm implements to producing half-track vehicles, deuce-and-a-half trucks, and parts to keep the army on the go.

Because of her brother's connections at Deere, Anna was offered a part-time position, which she appreciated, but turned down because with her recent promotion and a four-cent-an-hour raise, she didn't feel she needed to take away an opportunity for someone else who could use the job. The offer was a big deal because up until now, neither women nor Negros had been hired to work there. But the times now dictated a change to that policy. The demands from the defense department to meet their orders meant both were needed to fill the three shifts they were running.

Anna went into the house to retrieve the letter she had written to Jim so she could get it in the mailbox before the mailman came by. It had been over two week since Jim's last letter—the longest period between letters she had waited since he went back to Texas. She tried not to be concerned, but the news of the invasion made her a little anxious to hear from him.

She hoped the next letter might indicate or provide some information as to where he was and where he would be headed.

With the censorship, Jim could not provide a lot of detail of where he was or where he might be going. She knew only that he was in England and at some point had made it to London. Jim had indicated that he didn't care much for the weather, the food, or the coffee. He described London as a city that was not just in the war but was in the middle of a war zone. He had explained how the British people had suffered from the German air raids that came almost nightly. Jim wrote that the city was a very dark city where every light, including the street lamps, were covered to help conceal what the Germans would see when they attacked from the air.

Jim went on to say that the English were making sacrifices to the war, much like that which the Americans were doing; except in England, they were not rationing. In most cases, they would go without. They sacrificed items like gas, clothing, soap, food, wood for making furniture, and fresh vegetables. All these items and so many more were needed by their military to carry out the war effort. He described how most of the farm fields were being used to grow wheat, and the flower gardens were dug up and now grew vegetables for their soldiers. Jim said Britain appeared hard and tattered, not at all what the British people wanted to leave for a first impression to the Americans who had come to assist them in this effort. Jim said he was still impressed with the looming towers, the magnificent cathedrals and castles that were so old, so large, and so impressive.

Anna reached the mailbox that was set on a wooden post facing the street. She put the letter in the box, closed the lid and put the flag up. As she started back to the house, she glanced up to the sky to see a cloudless day as the sun was rising over the treetops. She wiped the perspiration from her brow with her apron as she softly said, "Maybe today, yes, I am sure I will hear from Jim today."

Chapter 14

THE PUSH THROUGH BELGIUM

The gun crews were at a standstill waiting for the weather to break when a jeep sped into the compound. A sergeant stood up in the back of the jeep, and as he started to open a large sack, he yelled, "Mail call."

The men hurried over as the sergeant started calling out names and tossing the letters in the direction of the response of "Yo." Jim got two letters from Anna and one from his dad. It had been seven days since anyone had seen any mail from home as finally the battalion was able to catch up with them.

They had spent little time in any one place as they were kept on the move. They would go from one town to another, where they would complete their fire missions, tear down, and move again. Now with the halt, the men were able to pause, sleep, and read their mail. Each man receiving a letter looked for a spot where they could be alone with the words written just for them. During this time, they could forget about the war and be with their family, even if that moment would be brief. It wasn't important what was written; it was just having a letter from home that made these times special. Each letter would be read and then carefully folded and put in a pocket so it could be pulled out and read again and again, at least until the next mail call.

Jim never threw a letter away. He kept each letter tucked away with his personal belongings as if they were a special treasure and a reminder of what was waiting for him once the war ended.

Summer had turned to fall, and fall was now giving way to winter as the Allied forces continued their push to rid France of the Germans. The 678th Battalion was bivouacked at Cambrai, France, when they finally got the orders to move to the front toward Belgium. They entered the town of Kortrijk which sat on the Leie River and was about fifty-two miles south of Brussels. Once they crossed the river and entered the town, they found that once again the Germans were committed to defending each city to keep it out of the hands of the invaders. Everywhere the men looked, they saw the destruction of the Germans who stubbornly fought, unwilling to yield anything that belonged to the Third Reich.

Between the artillery rounds and the bombers, every inch of this once quiet little town had been destroyed. The destruction was so great that again they had to wait for the rubble to be pushed aside to allow the advancing convoys through. It was becoming clear to each man as to how much the Europeans had had to endure during the early years of this war and how much it was going to cost to rid them of their German occupants.

There was not a building in sight that had been spared from this fight, as only hollow shells of what once was a building swayed, eventually giving way and tumbling to the rumbling of heavy equipment that passed by. Men were cautioned to stay away from and out of any building in the town because of how unstable they had become.

The moonless night made the passage uneventful as well as dangerous as they maneuvered their way through the city. The convoys of troops and equipment pushed forward, finally stopping on a hill which overlooked Oudenaarde. There was no time for rest as the gun crews quickly set up for their next mission. Each gun became ready and quickly reporting in.

"Gun one ready," McManis reported to the command.

"Stand by," came the order from Lieutenant Farr.

In the distance, the men could hear shell bursts and see tracer rounds lighting up the air as German planes had been detected in their area. Digger immediately took to digging a foxhole, but it wasn't long before each man was sitting on their equipment watching the bombardment as if it was a Fourth of July spectacle. They sat and applauded and shouted with each burst, but that ended when First Sergeant Johnson came over reminding them they were supposed to be standing by for a fire mission.

No shots were fired this evening as it was soon discovered that the Germans had no interest in holding on to the piece of property the battery was intent on blowing to hell. It was believed that the Germans had used the aircraft as a diversion, allowing them the time to escape. They had taken advantage of the same eerie cover of darkness the 678th used to gain their position without being detected, or so it was thought.

The battalion entered the city only to discover that somehow, some way, this little town had escaped the perils and destruction of this war. The advance party cleared the area and reported that there were no signs the Germans were ever there. As the convoy came in, the men noticed civilians. They made no gestures toward the advancing party, and the blank look on their face showed no signs of fear, joy, or hospitality. Over in a doorway, Jim noticed an older man, about the same age as his father, supporting himself on a cane as he stood on a wooden leg and watched. His eyes were sharp and suspicious as he followed their every move.

"McManis, your gun crew will occupy those buildings," said the first sergeant as he pointed to where the old man had been standing.

This would be the first time any of the members of their battery would be sleeping inside a building since they came ashore so many months ago.

The first sergeant went on to inform the men they were to spread their bedrolls anywhere they could find the space, but they were to stay out of the bedrooms. They were not to eat any of the civilians' food, even if it was offered, and were reminded to post a watch to keep an eye on the civilians during the night. Jim acknowledged the orders as he and the rest of the gun crew grabbed their gear and headed for the cottage.

As Jim, Lad, Otto, Chick, and Bobbie stepped through the archway of the door and entered the house looking around the room to see what kind of quarters they had drawn. It was a very simple design, with the kitchen to the right of the doorway. There was a wooden table and four chairs and a wood-burning stove that had a large metal container brewing some sort of stew or soup. The cupboards had no doors, so the contents were concealed by a small piece of fabric in front of each. Straight ahead of the entry was a large fireplace which had a fire burning. On the floor, there were a few stones which had a pot sitting on them, probably brewing apple cider. The floor was wood covered with a few handmade throw rugs, and in front of a rocking chair was a very old dog sound asleep. To the left of this room were two entries, again with no door, only a curtain that concealed the bedrooms.

The men walked over to the fireplace and placed their gear on the floor. The old man was in the kitchen standing next to his wife and daughter. As they stood close together, they carefully evaluated the soldiers' movement. Lad gestured by tipping his helmet and placing some chocolate bars on the table trying to reassure them that they only wanted the warmth of the fire and a place, other than outside, to sleep. A brief and nervous smile crossed the face of the daughter as she reached for the chocolate bars and placed them in her apron.

The old man walked across the room and picked up a few sticks of wood, tossing them into the fireplace. The older lady was in the kitchen tending to whatever she had on the stove. She had on a simple cotton dress and wore brown lace boots. Around her waist was an apron and on her head a scarf that hid most of her graying hair. The daughter, who was tending to the dishes, looked to be in her early twenties. She, too, wore a simple dress and boots. Her hair was coal black, and she wore it uncovered with the braids going down her back almost reaching her waist. Their faces revealed the years of hard work and the toil this war had on their lives. They went about their business as if the soldiers were not there, and it was just another evening meal, but the old man kept a watchful eye on their movement.

Jim, along with the other men, placed his gear in neat little piles next to where they spread their bedrolls. They removed their coats and sat down on the floor. Jim gathered the rations from each and placed them on the stone next to the fire to get them warm. As he waited for his supper to warm, he removed the liner from his helmet and sat it next to the fire. He poured water from his canteen into the helmet and took out his steel mess cup and put one packet of coffee grounds in it. He reached for his pipe and his pipe tobacco as he laid his head down on his butt pack.

It wasn't long before both the water and his meal were ready. Jim carefully opened the can and started enjoying spaghetti with meat sauce— an evening meal designed to provide a soldier with enough calories to sustain their activity as well as to provide the fuel they would need to keep their bodies warm. But tonight, they had the comfort of a floor, a roof over their heads, and the warmth of a fire.

After dinner, Jim walked outside to enjoy the silence of the evening. The moon was shining as if it were a flashlight guiding the visitors' footsteps as they guarded their post. As he glanced up at the sky, his thoughts turned to Anna. She would be just getting off work and heading home to attend to her evening meal. Jim cringed at the thought that she would have to tend with that old coal furnace to keep the house warm and hoped that maybe his dad was looking in on her this winter.

As he was lighting his pipe, he heard a bang and then a commotion coming from the house. He grabbed his carbine and quickly entered. As he went inside, the commotion had turned to laughter. He looked over to see Chick wiping beans off his shirt and face from the explosion of his supper. He let it sit too long by the fireplace. Jim looked into the kitchen to see both the mother and daughter attempting to hide the smiles they had on their face as they sat at the table. The father's expression had not changed, as he continued to sit with his head down eating his evening meal.

During this stay, the men took a much-needed break, and they received a visit from Major General Collins, commander of the Seventh Corps. The general made the trip to their site to visit the troops and to promote Major McDonald, who was the executive officer of the battalion, to lieutenant colonel. The men put on their best fatigues, shaved, and stood formation for the promotion ceremony and the ceremonial inspection of the troops. This consisted of the general, along with the battalion staff, walking briskly up and down, each formation glancing briefly at the troops. They were not really concerned with the appearance of the troops or the shine on their boots; they were just completing that which is always expected in a visit like this.

That evening, it started to snow; and Jim, along with the rest of the gun crew, started gathering their gear realizing that they would be moving out. A field artillery unit would become an easy target for any German artillery unit if they were to discover that the Americans were pinned down, unable to return fire, and sitting in a village.

Davidson walked over to the old man, handed him his pipe and tobacco, tipped his hat to the ladies, and walked out the door. Jim couldn't be sure, but he thought he actually saw the man smile as he looked down at the gift he held in his hand.

Jim caught up with Davidson and asked, "Was that all of your tobacco?" Lad answered, "Yes, it wasn't a big deal. Besides, the old man looked like he could use a good smoke once we left him alone."

Jim rubbed Lad on the head and said, "I've got plenty for both of us, at least for a little while."

The battalion hadn't been out of the village for more than an hour when they heard the distant sound of artillery rounds striking the village. The men wanted to stop and return fire, but their mission was in front of them. There was no time to stop or fight for ground they had already passed. The Germans had to know that the Americans had left and figured it was their way of punishing the once untouched village for the hospitality they had extended to them, as if they had any other choice.

As they made their way forward, Jim couldn't help but think of the comfort of their homes for the last few days and wondered what the hell they could have done to warrant this attack. As each round slammed the city, the men felt more helpless and angry until they heard the sound of English fighters coming in over their heads and attacking the area where the shelling was coming from. One after another, the planes dove down, dropping their bombs and strafing the gun crews with their fifty-caliber machine guns.

"I hope they kill all the bastards," Otto said as he pumped his fist in the air.

Each man watched silently as the planes continued their attack. Finally, after several passes, the planes rose in the sky blending in with the clouds and disappeared from their sight. It was done, and all that could be heard was the sound of their vehicles making their way in the freshly fallen snow, taking them to their next mission. The men would later learn that an air strike was called in by the newly promoted executive officer who also wanted to go back but knew they couldn't.

Company C led the way, staying about three miles in front of the battalion, looking for any signs of the enemy or areas that hadn't been cleared. For their protection, they had picked up a rifle platoon who had the job of assuring their passage was cleared and returning fire if they came in contact with a German patrol.

As the company entered into a wooded area, they drew fire from a sniper. All the track vehicles immediately stopped and returned fire, cutting down every limb that had hidden the location of the shooter. It wasn't long before a German soldier fell like a pinecone head first into the snow. The platoon sergeant from the rifle company, along with two of his men, cautiously approached the lifeless body. The blood coming from the wounds in his chest and head clearly signaled the end of the war for him. The members of the rifle platoon quickly fanned out and started moving through the area, making sure he didn't have a buddy or wasn't a lookout who had just warned his group of their arrival.

While the company stood alongside their vehicle waiting for the "all clear" sign, Captain Dallas noticed a pill box that did not have any marking, showing it had been cleared of booby traps. He, along with Lieutenant Farr, carefully advanced to the pillbox to confirm and mark it so others who passed would know it was safe. As they entered, they noticed a helmet and a swastika lying on the ground over by a soldier's butt pack and canteen. Before the captain could caution him, the lieutenant reached down; and as he picked up the helmet, it exploded, blowing the captain out the door and killing the lieutenant.

First Sergeant Johnson was the first to reach the captain who was bleeding from his left shoulder and had a large piece of the canteen protruding from his right leg.

"Medic!" the first sergeant yelled as he reached for his first aid pack and applied direct pressure over the captain's wounds. Once the medic arrived, the first sergeant entered the pillbox and carefully picked up the lieutenant's body. He brought him outside, laid him on the ground under a tree, and covered him with his poncho.

Davidson and Davis were the first men to reach the first sergeant. He looked at their faces and knew he needed them to focus on the danger still around them and not on the captain or the dead body lying in front of them.

"Check the area for any other booby traps you might find on the ground. If you find anything, mark it, but leave it lying," came the orders from the first sergeant who assumed command along with the responsibility for the safety of the company.

Davidson and Stinky were joined by the rest of the gun crews who walked in pairs, sifting through the snow carefully watching as they inspected the grounds for anything else the Germans may have left behind.

The rifle platoon, hearing the explosion, came rushing back into the area and saw what had happened.

"Plunger, I need you to get two gallons of diesel fuel and bring it here," barked the first sergeant.

Private Brooks did exactly what was asked, bringing up the cans from the back of their track vehicle and handing them over to the first sergeant.

Two other men from the battery got the body of the German who had been killed and put him inside the pillbox as directed, while the first sergeant doused the interior with the fuel. Once everyone, including the wounded captain and the lieutenant was at a safe distance, the first sergeant set the bunker on fire. The thick black smoke rose from the bunker filling the air and each soldier' nostrils with the strong order of the fuel, as well as the distinctive order of the burning flesh of the German. It was an odor like nothing the men had ever smelled before, and it would be a smell that would stay with them for the rest of their lives.

* * * *

Captain Dallas was alert and assumed his role as commander while they waited for the Battalion to join them. The medic had stopped the bleeding but did not remove the shrapnel, being concerned that removing it could cause an artery to bleed out that he couldn't stop. He had hung an IV with plasma, replacing the volume of blood the captain had lost, and he tried to give him a shot of morphine, which he refused because he didn't want anything to impede his thought process until he could be relieved of his duties.

As they waited for the battalion to join them, the snow had started to pick up, and the wind started to blow, making the visibility a little difficult to see through the wooded area.

"Get the men under cover and post a perimeter around us. We can't be sure if this area is clear, and we don't what to get caught in an ambush," the captain told First Sergeant Johnson.

The rifle company established the perimeter as the men from the gun crew attended to their equipment. They knew that these track vehicles could go about anywhere, but if the snow exceeded eighteen inches, they would be sitting ducks trying to pull these heavy guns.

Jim, Lad, Otto, and Max all found cover around a group of trees within feet of their gun. They cut the lower hanging branches and laid them on top of each other trying to provide a floor that would keep them off the wet snow that was now a blizzard. Once they had branches on the ground, they put their ponchos together, making a large lean-to facing away from the wind and the blowing snow.

"Do you suppose we can build a small fire for warmth?" Stinky asked.

Jim answered that it would be okay since the bunker was still ablaze. They gathered some small twigs, and with a little fuel, they started a fire. Jim removed his helmet and liner as they mixed their coffee and cocoa together to give them something warm to drink. They sat back and waited for the water to come to a boil as Jim took out his pipe, loaded the bowl, and without saying a word, handed the tobacco pouch over to Lad.

"Damn, I never gave it a thought that the captain would get it," said Otto. Lad lit his pipe and said, "Yes, he is a good man, and we are going to miss him and his guidance. I guess if there is any good news in all this at least the captain should be home for Christmas."

"Yeah, you're probably right, but if we were to ask him, I bet he would say he would prefer to be here with us," Jim muttered.

The men had seen casualties before, but this was the first time it happened to them, to one of their own. And even though they were not fond of the lieutenant, they couldn't help but to think of his family back in Texas. They figured the Red Cross would notify them right after Thanksgiving, which was just a day out.

At least they would not have to remember that thanksgiving was the day they lost their son, Jim said to himself.

Finally, the battalion joined up, bringing along their doctor, who started tending to the captain and getting him ready for his journey back to the aid station and eventually to a surgeon. The first sergeant was helping the medics load him on a track vehicle when Jim came over, lit a cigarette, and put it in the captain's lips.

"Thanks, Arky. Now you guys stop thinking of me and get this damn war over."

He looked at Jim. "When was the last time you shaved, soldier?" he said as he reached out and grabbed Jim's hand giving it a squeeze as if he wanted to make sure his men were okay before he departed the field. Next to the captain, they placed the body of the young lieutenant, who also had been placed on a gurney, wrapped in a poncho and tied down for the trip.

The snow had stopped, and the command came for the men to saddle up. They would keep fighting the elements as they pushed their way towards Brussels. There, they would once again pause so they could draw supplies, gasoline, ammunition, clothing, and food for the push through the Ardennes. General Omar Bradley and the First Army were pushing through the Ardennes, while General Patton, along with the Third Army, was moving in from the north.

The Ardennes were the logical choice for the field artillery units because they could set good defensive positions guarding the roads, overlooking the waterways, and moving from one area to another quickly if needed to support the advancing army. Their main objective was to prevent the Germans, who were attempting to resupply their army, from doing so, as well as preventing them from crossing back into Germany.

Chapter 15

AN ACT OF DESPERATION

The battalion finally reached Brussels in the early afternoon on Wednesday, December 5, 1945, looking to hook up with their next attachment. Not ever being assigned to a division, they were known as a bastard battalion going wherever they were needed, accomplishing their mission, and then moving on. Because they were always attached, they did not rest when the other division rested; they just moved to support another operation.

They had been in the field for over one hundred and thirty days, and this pause was a welcome stop even if it would be brief. They were looking forward to some hot chow, warm, dry clothing, and maybe a good night's sleep.

The outcome of this war was known as the Allied forces had the Germans on the run. They had finally gained air superiority over the German Luftwaffe, which was allowing them to run bombing missions over Germany every day. From the air, they were destroying the factories, railways, and facilities that the Germans had used to supply their army, thus destroying their ability to carry on this fight. In the field, Germans, who were trapped from escaping and unable to be resupplied, were forced to surrender by the hundreds, and things were going so well that rumors were circulating the war would be over by Christmas.

The next day most of the men took the opportunity to attend church services before heading over to a makeshift mess hall for an early Christmas feast.. On the menu was turkey with dressing, giblet gravy, cranberry sauce, snowflake potatoes, Irish baked corn, buttered pea, fruitcake, raisin pie, hot rolls, butter, jam, and coffee.

Jim sat down, glanced at all the food on his plate, and said, "Do any of you remember when we got a similar meal served to us on that British ship that brought us over here? I am sure this is going to be a hell of a lot better than that meal, even if it was prepared by our army cooks."

"Oh my god, yes, I can't imagine anyone destroying this meal like they did that day. I think they could take the flavor out of corn flakes," answered Lad as he shoved a large piece of turkey into his mouth.

"After this meal, I am going to find a place where I can either take a hot bath or a shower. I don't remember the last time we bathed other than a quick PB and B (pits, balls, and butt) sponge bath," chimed in Stinky.

Jim laughed and said, "Yes, it will be nice to find a place where I can actually wash some of these clothes using hot water and imagine being able to do your daily duty and not having to worry about being shot."

Otto looked serious and said, "Dear Mrs. McManis, we regret to inform you that your husband, Sergeant James Donald McManis, was killed while taking a dump in the woods in Belgium."

Lad laughed and said, "Just give me a good night's sleep and the chance to read the *Stars and Stripes* newspaper from cover to cover without interruption, and I will be a happy camper."

Their orders came in, and on December 10, they moved from the comforts of the village toward their position in the Ardennes forest.

They crossed the Meuse River and joined up in support of other units from the First Army. C Battery occupying space on a hill that overlooked Saint Vith, a small village about fifty-two miles south of Belgium. Here, they were to look for and fire on any German vessel that was traveling on the river attempting to move men and supplies to their army.

The weather was not cooperating with General Bradley's attempt to advance because it had grounded the air support they needed to secure the land they were attempting to gain. For the next week, the men of Battery C would have to come up with ways to break the boredom as they waited for the push to cross into Germany. By now, the men had become accustomed to the hurry-up-and-wait routine of the army. But with the heavy snow that covered the ground and temperatures that had plummeted to the freezing mark, it became difficult to just stand by. The nights had become so cold they dug trenches that would take them underground to a makeshift shelter. There, they could huddle and use the soil, their blankets, ponchos, and anything else they had to keep them from freezing.

Several times a day, you would find the men doing jumping jacks, running in place, or other activities just to raise their body temperature. The trick was to do enough exercise to get warm without breaking into a sweat that would then eventually freeze. Men who had grown mustaches had them freeze to their upper lip from the moisture of their breath as they tried to carry out their duties. Most of the casualties at this point were from frostbite, especially to their hands and feet. With the nights being so dark from the overcast skies, they had to mark the trails to the makeshift latrine, the commander's area, ammo and fuel dump, and the first-aid station just to get around.

"Holy shit, does the sun ever shine on this godforsaken hell hole?" Wheeler said as he entered the trench. "What I wouldn't give to be back in Montana riding my quarter horse, checking the fence line, and whipping the sweat from my brow."

"Cowboy, you can have the horse. I am thinking about the warm sand pushing through my toes as I run along the beach in California," answered Hollywood. "Here, I made some hot soup and coffee for all of us."

"How in the hell did you do that?" asked Wheeler.

"I traded with an infantry man—two pairs of socks for this plastic explosive. It only takes a small piece. It burns hot, gives off no fumes, and as long as you don't step on it, we can use it to heat things up," Chick answered.

Wheeler looked at the soup and said, "You gave away your socks? Are you nuts?"

Chick laughed and said, "Well, I am nuts because I am here but not stupid. They were from Lieutenant Farr's clothing issue, and I didn't think he would mind."

On the morning of December 16, the men were awakened by the sound of field artillery shells and buzz bombs striking at the edge of their position. They looked for and took cover as the shells came closer. There was much confusion as to what was happening because there had been no intelligence report of any activity by the Germans and nothing reporting they had the capability to launch an assault. But from the pounding they were taking, that is what they were under.

Jim and Lad launched themselves into the bunker Otto had made, and for the first time since this war started, they were glad Digger had dug. As the shells fell around them, the fire burst that was lighting up the morning sky painted an orange glow on the low-hanging fog. The strong odor of gunpowder filled the area as each man could only sit and wait for it to end. They knew everything would be fine as long as they could hear the sounds of the incoming buzz bombs, but once it stopped, they waited for impact, knowing all anyone could do was get down, take cover, and pray it didn't have your name on it.

As Jim looked out through the cracks in the timber, which made up their roof, he saw the shells striking the treetops, scattering limbs, bark, and branches like it was being blown around by a tornado. Just as Jim loosened the strap from his helmet, a shell landed next to their cover sending large chunks of dirt, snow, and debris into the sky. A small piece of shrapnel glanced across Jim's forehead right above his left eye. The percussion of the explosion knocked Jim's helmet off his head, and as he reached to recover it, he felt blood flowing down his head and into his eye. Jim wiped at his eyes as he strained to look out on the field. He could see men scrambling to find cover to escape the debris flying through the air. As Jim watched, everything started to slow down, and the sounds of the explosions seemed distant. Men were yelling for exposed soldiers to take cover as the shells kept coming in. Jim watched a man from Gun Three running across the open field, and as he jumped into his foxhole, a shell hit. All he heard was the explosion as the content from the foxhole was tossed in the air. Jim saw the smoke drifting from the impact area, and the only evidence that there was a human life in the rubble was the red blotches of blood that were splattered over the snow.

Jim felt the hands of Lad who quickly applied pressure to his wound from his first-aid pouch. As Lad finished wrapping Jim's head, he said, "There you go, Arky. It's just a flesh wound, but you will need to keep the pressure on until you can see the medic and get a couple of stitches."

"Thanks, Davidson. Is everyone else okay?" inquired Jim.

"Yeah, we kept our head down," Otto said as he handed Jim his helmet. The bombardment lasted for more than thirty minutes as the men sat inside with their own thoughts. Finally, the guns moved to another area; and as they became more distant, the men came out from their cover. Each looked around, surveying the damage. To their surprise, they discovered that somehow they had only lost the one soldier, the man Jim had seen running in front of him. Three guns from the battalion and two of the M5 track vehicles had been destroyed. But to everyone's amusement, the only area that took the most direct hit was the latrine. There was frozen shit thrown everywhere.

As the men were looking around, a report came in for a fire mission. Lieutenant Parker, an air observer, reported that he was flying over a large-scale assault of Panzers and infantry that were quickly advancing on the Ninety-ninth Infantry Division. They needed immediate cover, or they would be overtaken.

They readied the guns and began to fire. The forward observer called in adjustments until finally, when the Germans were within two hundred yards of overrunning the Ninety-ninth, the guns were on target. The 678th poured it on, pounding the area with over one hundred and seventy-five rounds striking and stopping the advancing army in their tracks. The Panzers that survived the strike were forced to turn away from the Americans, allowing them to take on the German infantry and hold their position.

The 324th Combat Engineer Battalion made its way back to the tree-covered area where the 678th had been firing from. Jim and the members of his gun crew watched as the men came in, slapping them on the back and telling them how much they appreciated getting them out of that jam.

"You guy's blew the hell out of them. That was some of the best shooting I have seen in this war," one private said, as he looked for an area to set up his gun placement.

Jim smiled and said to Davidson, "Maybe this makes up for those other infantry men we didn't cover."

Lad said, "Arky, I think we made a difference, more often than we know."

The private went on to tell the story of how the spotter plane calling in the strike was hit by small arm fire just as it was climbing to get out of harm's way. He said the plane rolled to its left and then fell from the sky, exploding on impact. He said they watched for parachutes, but neither of the men got out. Jim didn't know these two officers personally, but he realized all the praise the men had for their performance actually belonged to Captain Rice and second Lieutenant Isham who were making the adjustments for their fire mission. The families of both these men would later be awarded the Silver Star and the Purple Heart posthumously for their heroic efforts.

The engineers took over the area as the 678th received orders moving them back toward the Meuse River. As they were withdrawing to their new position, they had to occasionally pull off the road, giving way to the advancing American tanks that were speeding to provide additional support for the Ninety-ninth who were just holding on.

The frozen ground provided good traction as they heard the sound of the battle. From a distance they could hear the sounds of German Panzers that had turned and were trying to assault the middle of the Allied lines. With the cloud cover, the Germans knew that the Allied air support would be of no use, and they were assaulting with everything they had in the area. The Fifth Panzer Army, led by General Manteuffel, was attacking the center of the American forces. Their plan was to capture the strategic roads and rails of Saint Vith and then drive on to Brussels. The Sixth Panzer Army, led by General Sepp Dietrich, was leading the attack with the intent to capture Antwerp.

Hitler believed that this assault would allow his forces to surround and cut off Canada's First Army, America's First and Ninth Armies, and Britain's Second Army. He used his armored forces to attack, which he believed would allow them to quickly overrun the Allied positions, preventing them from retreating or conducting a counterattack. The Panzers moved quickly through the area with the majority of the German armored might based at the Schnee Eifel. The Germans experienced great success in the beginning of this operation.

The Allies were completely caught off guard by this attack. They had received little intelligence that such an attack would or could even take place. On the eve of the attack, English-speaking German soldiers who wore American uniforms went behind the lines and created confusion for the Allies by passing out misinformation, changing road signs, and cutting telephone lines. The weather was in Hitler's favor with low cloud cover and fog that prevented the Allies from using their tank-busting typhoons of the RAF or Mustang fighter aircraft. Much of this battle would be affected by the weather. Great snowstorms became a big problem, slowing down supplies, fuel, fresh troops, and ammunition. Trucks were started and ran every half hour to keep the oil from freezing. The men's individual weapons would freeze up, so men would urinate on their weapon to thaw them so they could be used. The temperatures were the coldest on record, and casualties from exposure from the cold were higher than the ones from the fighting.

In two days, the Germans had pushed the Allied lines in the middle causing them to bulge, a name the contemporary press would use when they called it the "Battle of the Bulge." Despite punching a bulge into the Allies' front line, the Germans did not capitalize on their advance and soon found themselves out of fuel. Many of the Panzer division soldiers simply could not continue, so they got out of their tanks and started walking back toward Germany.

The weather cleared on the twenty-second of December, and the Allies were able to get the air wings involved in the action.

U.S. troops and some British troops counterattacked to eliminate the Bulge. The U.S. First Army, under General Bradley, was attacking from the north; and General George Patton, who had made remarkable time moving his division down to the fight, led his Third Army from the south. Patton quickly broke through, freeing the 101st Airborne unit that was under siege at Bastogne. In the face of increasing Allied pressure, the Germans began to withdraw from the Bulge on January

8, 1945. The Americans started to move, eliminating all of the German gains.

This was the largest fight carried out by the American Army during the entire European conflict. It encompassed over one million men from both sides. The U.S. Army was outmanned and outgunned during this campaign. Casualties from the conflict would vary as to the number, but American casualties were reported to be from seventy thousand to eighty-one thousand, with over half of those suffering from frostbite. The British had fourteen thousand reported casualties, and the German losses were between sixty thousand to over one hundred thousand, with an additional one hundred thousand becoming prisoners of war. In addition to the human loss, there were over seven hundred tanks lost on both sides and as many as one thousand German aircraft destroyed, thus ending any effort Hitler might have had to carry on this fight by air or by land.

On January 8, 1945, the 678th received orders taking them back across the Meuse River and advanced toward Germany. As they made their way through the Ardennes, they saw evidence of the battle that had taken place. The bodies of the dead had not yet been moved by Graves Registration. There were frozen bodies everywhere you could see. Each looking more like ice sculptures than soldiers revealed the costly consequences of this fight.

Jim looked in all directions and asked himself, "For what? What did they think they were going to do here besides die?"

Everywhere Jim looked, he saw tanks—most of them destroyed and still smoldering—but many just abandoned, sitting like they were hibernating waiting for the warmth of spring to stir them back to life.

Chapter 16

CROSSING INTO GERMANY

The weather was breaking, and the warmer temperatures were melting the snow and slowing the progress of the battalion as the guns started to bog down in the mud and slush. The track vehicles were able to maneuver through the terrain without much difficulty, but the guns were another subject. They either would get stuck, requiring the men of the crew to get off and walk alongside and push, or they would slide from side to side on and off the road. Finally, the battalion stopped, and each battery was tasked with building toboggans for their guns to sit on.

A toboggan, unlike a sled, would be the best choice to pull the heavy guns through the wet and slushy snow. With a toboggan, the pressure per square inch of ground contact area is less than a sled. So they would not bury or plow, which allowed the track vehicles to pull their load easier and with less risk that the gun would slide away or turn over.

It was getting close to dusk once the men had the toboggans built and the guns mounted. They decided to pull off the road and bivouac in the small wooded area just large enough for their needs. The men were told this was not going to be a cold camp, Allowing them to build small fires, something they had not enjoyed in a very long time. Each battery would set up its mess tent for dinner, and there would be both hot chow and hot coffee.

Jim went over to the battalion aid station to have his dressing changed before heading to the mess tent for fresh coffee and maybe a snack, if the bakers had anything left.

"You're going to be fine, Sergeant," said the medic. "The wound is healing fine, and the stitches are still in tact. I will need to see you in a couple of days to remove them. Are you having any problems with headaches, dizziness, vomiting, or any vision difficulties?" the medic inquired.

"Nope, I am fine," Jim answered, "just looking forward to some hot chow and maybe some hot water to shave with."

As Jim stood up, he said, "Thanks, kid. I really appreciate you taking care of me. I will see you in a couple of days."

He ducked under the tent flap and walked outside.

Jim glanced up to discover the old moon had made a rare but much appreciated appearance in the evening sky. The light it was providing was making it a lot easier to find his way around the compound. Just as he looked back down he felt a thump on his back.

"Hey, Arky, mind if we join you?"

Jim looked over his shoulder to discover Stinky Davis and Anthony. "So when do you suppose they will give you your Purple Heart?" Davis asked.

"Purple Heart?" Anthony piped up. "Are you nuts? They don't give those things out for cutting yourself shaving?"

Jim chuckled and said, "Come on, Stinky, you can buy me and Yankee a cup of hot Joe!"

The battalion headed northeast as they made their way to catch up with Patton's Third Army, which was making a dash toward Germany. On February 3, they crossed into Germany and sat outside the small village of Aachen. The city lay in nearly complete ruins just like so many cities they had seen before. There was no reason to stop, so they pushed on until they reached the hills overlooking Heistern. There, the batteries would spread out and prepare for their first fire mission on German soil.

They had to hold their position at Heistern as the entire force was being held up, waiting for the waters to recede because the Germans had blown up the dams. They had become used to these tactics the Germans often deployed to slow down or delay the Allied advance, in their case the push toward Cologne. Intelligence reports could not confirm or deny if the Germans had used the flooding to escape or to dig in for a fight.

On February 23, the waters finally receded enough, allowing the American infantry to start their crossing of the Roer River. From the west side of the river, the 678th opened up with a massive barrage of fire to provide cover and strike-targeted areas intelligence indicated the Germans were expected to be. The fire coverage only lasted long enough to allow the first wave to get ashore. As they fanned out and secured Duren, they found only pockets of resistance, which were quickly isolated and destroyed. Within a few hours of the assault, the area was considered secured. With the fire mission complete and the area secured, the batteries once again prepared to follow the heavy armor across the river and on to Cologne.

They came into a farming village called Geilrath. There, they made their first contact with German civilians. An old woman close to the vicinity of Battery B was captured. Her apparent mission was to take care of the cattle that were now scattered all over the countryside. The cows appeared to be suffering as much as any animal they had seen up to this point. With most of the locals gone, the cows obviously had not been milked for some time. Those members of the battalion who had been raised on a farm quickly fanned out into the fields to attend to the cows. Scattered throughout these fields were the carcasses of dead and decaying cows. Many had starved to death, and some probably couldn't take the cold suffering any longer. The flies were so thick that from a distance, it looked like a cloud was hanging over each dead animal. Worse was the smell coming from the decaying bodies as well as the manure that covered the field. In order for the men to get to the animals, they had to cover their face with anything they had.

They went about their business of allowing their skilled hands to relieve the cows of their burden and reap the reward of their work by providing the men of the battalion with fresh milk.

The milk was distributed to each battery, and it didn't take long before the milk had chilled enough for the men to enjoy. Each man filled his canteen cup and sat back enjoying rare treat. They looked like school children who had just come in from play as they slowly sipped on the sweet taste of the chilled beverage. Without comment, they smiled as each savored the delight of such a simple pleasure. Who would you have imagined that these hardened men could take such delight in a simple glass of milk?

Otto wiped the milk mustache from his upper lip and said, "Who would have thought a glass of milk could halt an army?"

Jim laughed as he thought about the faces of the children who used to be so excited when they saw him on his old milk run back in Iowa.

"Yeah, but who is going to burp you when you're done?" asked Davis. Each village was the same as they made their way toward Cologne. The destruction of this war was going to be felt long after it had ended. One had to wonder if many of these small communities would even be rebuilt. Would they stand as a reminder for the generations to come of the stupidity of man and the cost for his quest for power, or would they quickly rebuild with the hope of erasing this horror from the next generations who would live there?

On March 3, the battalion moved into Glessen, another village that had suffered from the ravages of this war. This time, the battalion encountered Germans still living in their homes. They seemed eager to please the Americans by offering them their homes and beds, washing the men's clothing, and providing other services which would include information on the location of the German Army and the direction they were heading.

They men were reminded that there would be no fraternization allowed. "Do not get friendly with the locals," First Sergeant Johnson went on to say.

"I know you haven't seen a woman in some time, and you may feel a need to spend some time with one, as they can become real friendly. But you need to remember, that in the eyes of the army, they are our enemy, and if you are caught sleeping with one, I will have you court martialed for fraternization. Is that clear?"

He went on to say, "Assume the only reason for their hospitality is because they are afraid of being shot, a trick the Nazis used in order to gain submission. And they think we are capable of doing the same. Is that understood?"

Anthony looked into the face of one younger man and said, "These Germans are not hard to get along with. I mean, after you kick their ass and you hold a gun on them, they seem to be real pleasant people."

Lad took exception to that comment and barked back, "Knock it off, Yankee. They are probably as sick of this damn war as anyone. How long do you think they have suffered under the threat of being shot? I would imagine they just want to go back to their life and to be left alone so they can go about their business of raising a family and living in peace."

"Well, maybe they should have thought of that before they started this fucking mess," Anthony snapped.

"I doubt anyone asked them for their opinion" came the reply from Davidson as he grabbed his carbine and walked away.

"What's eating him?" asked Davis.

Jim watched Lad as he walked away and said, "Stinky, maybe he looks at them and sees our families and realizes how lucky we are that this war is far away from them."

On March 6, the 678th Battalion had made its way through Widdersdorf and was within sight of the Cologne cathedral and the Hohenzollern bridge across the Rhine. From a distance, the men could see this magnificent building standing alone with the steeple reaching up from the rubble to the heavens, as if it was holding the hand of God. The large stained glass windows appeared to be intact, and from their viewpoint, the only thing missing were those who would worship there.

"How in the name of God did the American and British bombers miss such a large structure as that?" Plunger asked.

"Exactly, it was in the name of God" came the response from Hollywood. "Maybe it's a symbol that even in war we can find hope in God's house." Lad and Jim looked at each other, somewhat taken aback by Chick's comments, as this was a side they had not seen before.

Jim realized it was a process that each of them would go through. How do you deal with the killing, the destruction, and the worst of mankind that only a war can bring out of a human and still remain faithful to the teachings of God?

They would not stand there long as news came that the Allied forces had captured the Ludendorff bridge intact, and they were being moved, not across the Rhine as first planned but back through Belgium, France, and Luxembourg to Woelfling. It would be a three-hundred-twenty-five mile detour away from where they thought they would be going. There was no reason to ask why. The army doesn't make a habit of explaining the reasons behind the orders; you're just expected to comply with the orders you have been given. As they made the preparation for the move, there was one thing they all knew. Today, they would not be crossing the Rhine River. That was an event that would have to come on another day.

On March 17, Saint Patrick's Day, the division moved out of the village of Woelfling after a day of heavy shelling, once again crossing into Germany. The battalion crossed the fields that were damaged from the shell bursts the previous day only to find them littered with enemy dead. As they made their way toward the quiet little town of Gersheim, they paid little attention to the destruction they had caused and even less attention to the souls that lay motionless waiting for someone to bury them.

Jim glanced at the faces and felt nothing. He wondered if the war had made him so callous and if it had become so commonplace that it no longer had any effect on him. Had he lost his compassion for human life, or like so many who were fighting, did he understand that they had no other options if they were to end this damned war?

There was little time for thought as they quickly passed through Gersheim. Not to anyone's surprise, there wasn't a civilian to be found in the village as it had apparently been abandoned for some time. As they approached the town of Breitfurt, there was a hill that was heavily fortified and being held by the Germans. A bastion of Germans from the Siegfried line were dug in and protected by pill boxes, which would provide them with good cover from an aerial attack.

The only effective way to silence these guns was to put artillery fire directly on the target. Battery C drew the short straw and advanced to their position. Normally, the batteries were well behind the front line supporting the infantry. But this mission required them to be in front to find the targets and destroy them prior to the infantry movement to clean up any pockets of resistance that might be left.

They were supported by Company C of the First Infantry Division as they took their positions. The infantry's job was to keep any Germans who might be in the area off their back so the field artillery units could concentrate on the fire mission. As the guns were being placed and the firing stakes laid, the forward observer moved out to seek cover that would allow him to see the target and adjust the fire. All guns were ready as they waited for their next command. Suddenly, from their left flank, they drew small arms fire. The infantry took position and, for the next fifteen minutes, exchanged fire until the Germans either lie dead or had withdrawn.

They believed this was a small patrol whose purpose was to identify any Allied movement and report back to their headquarters. Why they engaged the unit was a mystery, but they could take no chances that some of them got away and that their position had been compromised.

There was no time to move to another sight as Jim radioed in "Gun One ready."

Lad cut the powder and shoved the sack into the chamber behind the projectile that had been armed and readied. Chick and Davis continued to open the crates and prepare each round that was to be fired and passed it forward.

They would be firing highly explosive shells that on impact would destroy the concrete barriers the Germans were hiding in. Gun One fired the first round, followed by each of the four guns in the battery.

After each gun fired, they made their normal adjustments based on the information called back to them by the observer.

Finally, after each gun had fired only three rounds, the command came in. "Fire at will."

Round after round slammed into the mountain side. The fire and explosions were so intense that, even with them being a good four miles away, they felt the impact as the earth shook beneath their feet. After a few rounds, the gun had to be reset from the recoil of the projectile that came from its tube and was ready to continue the mission.

They kept up the barrage of the shelling strike, bunker after bunker, until the order came in. "Cease-fire."

All around the guns laid the brass casings that were ejected once the round was launched. The battery had collectively fired over three hundred and thirty rounds at these targets, leaving little doubt of the outcome. They quickly policed their brass and waited for the next set of orders, assuming they could stand down and wait for the infantry division to advance.

As the rest of the infantry division was on the move and just as the forward observer came in, they once again drew small arms fire. This time, the Germans were positioned on both sides of the battery and were advancing on their front. The infantry, with the help of the battery, quickly countered the attack. This firefight lasted over the next hour as the advancing division, who had heard the fire, quickly assaulted the Germans' flank, trapping them from any escape.

Several white phosphorus grenades were thrown at the automatic weapons placements that were assaulting with rapid fire. Those who were not killed on impact lay screaming as the chemical burned through their clothing and exposed skin like a rash that only grew more intense with the exposure. The only treatment for the exposure was to cover it and then have it scraped from the skin. Eventually, the rest of the German company gave up, realizing they had no other choice. It was either spend the rest of the war in a POW camp or spend the rest of eternity there in some shallow grave.

The medics quickly went to work identifying and treating the wounded on both sides. They did what they could as they went from man to man dressing the wounds and trying to make them comfortable. A medic didn't care about the uniform; they treated each man with precision and skill.

They saw an injury as a direct challenge to their skills and took pleasure in cheating death because too often the tools used to wage war made their job impossible.

The battery did not escape the attack, losing two men and having three others wounded.

Donald Wheeler was hit in the right shoulder. The round entered right above the collarbone, went through, and collapsed a lung as it shattered his shoulder. Plunger took a round in his ass as he dove for cover under the howitzer. His wound was superficial, and except for the countless ribbing he would take, he would be just fine. First Sergeant Johnson and two other members in the battery received wounds; none of which was life threatening.

Killed was First Lieutenant Donavan, the officer who replaced Lieutenant Farr. He was shot right above the left eye. The round had entered from the front and then exploded out the back of his head, scattering skull fragments, bones, and brains next to where he lay.

The other casualty was a nineteen-year-old new recruit who reported to the battery the same time as the lieutenant. He lay flat on his back, face up with his eyes open. His boyish blue eyes looked as if he was just watching the sun that was breaking through the cloud. He looked at peace, and the only sign of his wound was the small pool of blood that soaked his uniform from the round that ripped through his chest, piercing his heart.

Anthony watched as the medic gave Wheeler a second shot of morphine and saw Cowboy grimacing in pain as the medic applied new dressings to the already blood-soaked bandage he was using trying to get the bleeding to stop. Without saying a word, Yankee stood up, grabbed his carbine, and walked right toward a German sitting on the ground with his fingers locked behind his head. He pulled back the bolt of the riffle, placed a round in the chamber, and stuck it against the Germans head as he started yelling at him and prepared to pull the trigger.

First Sergeant Johnson, despite his wounds, knew the outcome if Yankee pulled that trigger. He said in a soothing tone, "Yankee, is he worth it? Do you want to spend the rest of your life in prison for killing him?"

"What the fuck are you talking about, Top? Isn't this what we get paid to do? Rid the earth of shit like this?"

"No, corporal," Johnson said, "he is a prisoner of war now, and if you pull that trigger, you become like him, and you lose your dignity, your humanity, and your freedom."

Anthony paused as his finger slid back and forth across the trigger. He looked at the first sergeant's face as he slowly lowered his rifle and walked back toward his wounded buddy. The first sergeant looked in the face of the German as he lit a cigarette and stuck it in his mouth. As he started to walk away, he glanced down to notice a large wet spot on the soldier's pants and ground where he had just pissed himself.

Chapter 17

IT IS OVER

By now, the Third Army was starting their push into Central Germany and onto Berlin. The enemy was withdrawing across the Rhine and far beyond—all while the Allies were in pursuit. The 678th kept on the move going from one German town to another, finally arriving in Enkenbach where they would pause to resupply and rest for a few hours. Once again, the men from Battery C discovered a local wine cellar with large quantities of famed Rhein and Moselle wines as well as an assortment of champagne.

The village was full of German civilians, and to the surprise of all, the locals were not as unfriendly as one might have expected, considering the circumstances. They shared their wines and were very hospitable toward the invaders by opening their homes, shops, and community to the men. Jim, Otto, and Lad decided they would partake in the beverages later, but for now, they wanted to borrow some bikes they had discovered, stretch out their legs, and enjoy the springlike day as they took in the countryside. There was a warm soft breeze coming in from the north that was making the ride very enjoyable—that is before they encountered an unarmed German soldier standing in the road with his hands in the air. Otto immediately jumped off his bike and drew his side arm, while Jim and Lad went to the side of the road not sure what was actually going on and looked to see if he had any friends waiting for them. The German, who spoke perfect English, said he was not armed and that he wanted to give up as he was tired and didn't want to fight for a useless cause anymore.

Otto kept him in his sight as Lad went through his pockets and tied his hands behind his back using the shoestring from his boot. Jim was some distance away keeping watch on the road. It was then that Jim turned and saw some movement in the tree line a few yards to his left.

"Halt! Place your hands in the air and come out slowly," Jim commanded as he removed the safety from his carbine and kept a close eye on the soldiers who were approaching him. One by one, they started coming out of the wooded area and onto the road. There were well over one hundred as they slowly came and sat down as Jim had instructed them to do. According to the first POW, they had been at this location for the last four days.

He went on to say they could have surrendered to an infantry unit that was in the area a couple of days ago, but they weren't sure if they were actually Americans or the gestapo pretending to be Americans. This was a tactic the Germans had deployed to prevent their soldiers from surrendering. If caught, they would have been shot on the spot. This time, they figured the gestapo wouldn't be out on a bike, so they decided to take the chance.

Now the relaxing day Jim thought they were going to enjoy had become a big problem. There was no way the three of them could spend the time to search each soldier, record all the items they took from them, secure the area, and get them off the road and back to the battalion. It was also going to be dangerous to stay here, knowing that other Germans could be in the area. They decided that they would move them out of this area and back toward the garrison. Once they were a thousand meters out, they would halt and have them sit in groups where the two of them could watch while the other would ride his bike back to the battalion to get assistance. Once the battalion was informed of the situation, they could bring up the support so the prisoners could be handled properly.

The three men drew straws, and Lad got the honors of racing back to the battalion. Jim and Otto had the task of standing guard and keeping the prisoners from talking.

"Here, take these three packs of cigarettes I have. With what you and Otto have," Lad explained, "it should keep their hands visible until I can get back."

Jim thought it strange that they did not have any weapons on them, so he turned to the interrupter and asked, "Where are your weapons?"

The German pointed toward the woods and said, "We have properly stacked them over there so you can have them. We have no need for them, and all we really want is to eat."

Otto looked at the German and asked, "What made you guys want to start this fight anyway?"

The German lit a cigarette, blew out a smoke ring, and answered, "You ever hear of the gestapo? Why did you join?"

Jim laughed and said, "Have you ever heard of the draft board?"

The big German smiled and nodded his head. "Well, I pray it will be over for all of us soon."

Jim heard the engines as five deuce-and-halves came rolling up the road with military police equipped to take over the task of processing these men and getting them to a secure place and some food. Jim and Otto handed over everything they had gathered, told them of the weapons that were stored, and started their ride back to the village.

While most of the men from their battery were enjoying the different wines and food from the village, Jim, Otto, and Lad were briefing the command on the circumstances leading up to and the actual details of the surrender of the one hundred sixteen Germans. By the time the briefing was complete, the only thing left for the trio was a good night's sleep.

Three more times the 678th would get close to the Rhine River, but each time their crossing would be delayed as they received new movement orders to support some other operation. But on Easter Sunday, April 1, 1945, in the early afternoon, they started their descent down the steep hills. They passed terraced vineyards, castles, and picture-book scenery as they slowly made their way down the winding roads. Once at the river, Jim looked out to see U.S. Navy boats patrol the river with the Stars and Stripes waving, a sight no one could have imagined as they approached the area. The day was getting late, so it was determined that they would stop, bivouac, and cross with the light of the next day.

As the sun rose, the much-anticipated crossing started. They crossed the Rhine without any incidents and took position in the hills overlooking Feudingen. For the next four days, the batteries fired over twelve hundred rounds striking the town, tanks, mortar positions, and personnel where the Germans were trying to hold on. These fire missions were so effective that it allowed the infantry to make a rapid advance, driving the Germans into a pocket where they would be surrounded completely by the Allied forces. To the south and west were the Americans and British forces. North and east were the Russians. There was no place for the Germans to go; they either had to stand and fight or surrender.

The battle that was pursued would be called the Ruhr pocket. It was beyond anyone's possible belief or anything the men of the 678th had ever seen since entering the war. The front line was constantly moving, and it was impossible to know if you were in the lead or following.

It was believed they had around one hundred thousand German troops trapped. That number would later be adjusted to over three hundred thousand. The Germans were unaware of the thinness of some of the Allied lines or the frantic movement that made their forces easy targets for a counterattack which would have allowed them to break through and escape. Instead, they stood and fought; but with little resolve to continue the fight, they mostly gave up.

Again, because of the fear of the gestapo, they would surrender to whomever passed by the second time. At Hosinghausen, the men of 678th Field Artillery would have to pause so they could process one hundred forty-one Germans who came out of the wooded area to give up as the battalion passed by. Among those surrendering were eight officers, a payroll, and a box marked secret, which was immediately turned over to headquarters for evaluation.

As the men from each battery searched the captives, they would identify and mark everything they found and whom it came from, just in case someone from intelligence needed to interrogate the soldier further.

First Sergeant Johnson told the men they did not need to take away the Germans' cigarettes or matches, but they were to remove all other items.

"Hey, Top," Jim asked, "do you mind if I keep this red swastika arm band and a set of wings for my scrap book?"

First Sergeant Johnson paused, looked back at Jim. "Hell, I don't care. He isn't going to need them, and I imagine the boys in intelligence already have some," he said as he turned and continued observing the men to ensure the treatment they were giving to their captives was within the military protocol for POWs.

"Remember men," the First Sergeant yelled out so all could hear, "they are soldiers just like you. They are to be treated as such. Don't take your eyes off them, don't trust them, but also don't mistreat them.

They are POWs, and we will treat them in accordance with the Geneva Convention that we all signed when we joined this man's army."

For the next several days, the battalion moved through towns like Birkelbach, Netphen, Dahlbruch, Kruber, Schwelm, Hosinghausen, Listernohl, and Hattingen. Names they would never remember, only the incidents that may have occurred, like a spigot left on allowing the wine to flow ankle deep in a cellar. Towns still were burning as they passed through, and Jim caught sight of a church sitting on a hill with a large shell hole blown clean through it.

"Hey, Lad," Jim said. "Now that is my kind of church, it's holey." "Arky, where do you come up with this shit?" Davidson asked as he looked over to the church, shook his head, and smiled.

They finally halted at Langenburg where two girls met them in a doorway wearing only a smile and holding two bottles of schnapps. It was hard to remember the fraternization rule, but with the help of the officers and a few MPs, the girls were quickly hustled away from the bivouac area.

Hollywood watched as the girls were covered up and led away. He turned to no one in particular and said, "Did you see the rack on those girls?"

"How in the hell could you miss them?" answered Stinky.

Davis went on and said, "I bet them damn officers keep those bottles of schnapps!"

"The hell with the schnapps. I would like to be the MPs," remarked Hollywood.

Davis laughed and said, "Hollywood, you might want to get your mind wrapped around something else or you probably won't be sleeping very well tonight."

On April 13, the men were informed that there was a battalion formation scheduled for 1400 hours. The rumors were circulating that the war was over and that Germany had surrendered. But to the surprise and disbelief of every man, it wasn't that at all. Colonel Dawson, commander of the 678th Field Artillery, stepped in front of the formation as the men were called to attention. He was holding a document in his hands and read the following message without hesitation or pause. "At 1330 hours yesterday, April 12, President Franklin D. Roosevelt died of a massive cerebral hemorrhage at his retreat in Warm Springs, Georgia. Harry S. Truman is now our president and commander-in-chief. That is all."

Many of the men just stood there in total disbelief. Roosevelt was the only president most of these men could remember. He had first been elected president in 1932 when these men were just young boys.

"Who in the hell is Harry Truman?" asked Yankee. "I don't remember hearing anything about him in school back in Adams, Massachusetts."

Well, I guess he was the vice president and our boss now," said Jim. That day was going to be no different from so many they had already had. Within a couple of hours since the announcement, they were on the move again.

From April 12 through April 29, they moved, fired, and moved again. They passed through town after town, many that had not been touched by the war. If it weren't for the American Army, there would have been no evidence that there was a war going on. The German people went about their daily lives as the battalion paused. They were polite and hospitable, treating the soldiers as if they were tourists there on holiday. Because of the friendliness of the civilians, fraternization started to become a concern. So watches and sentry duties were increased, especially during the evening hours to prevent any trouble.

The one village that Jim would remember was Mulheim. It was virtually untouched. There were large fruit trees for as far as the eye could see, and they were starting to bloom. Most of the families had large gardens in their backyards and shrubs lining their property like one would expect to see in a tourist guide. Here, there was no war, and the front seemed hundreds of miles away. It was just a small German town where the people went about their lives as if the soldiers weren't even there.

One afternoon, they had their guns in place overlooking another small village, waiting to see if they were going to receive a fire mission. Bobbie Wagner came up with the idea of cooking a goose he had gotten back at the last village. Wagner said he had spotted a small shack sitting just a few hundred yards to the left of their gun, and he would get the bird in the oven if they could cover for him.

The boys of Gun One were sitting quietly, waiting for either a mission or dinner when all of a sudden they saw the thick black smoke coming from the shack. It wasn't coming from the chimney but was coming from the shack, which was on fire. Jim immediately called the battery commander to say their gun was out of order as the others ran to the fire. As they arrived, they started throwing dirt on the flames calling for Wagner to get the hell out of there.

All of a sudden, with no sense of urgency, out walked Cookie holding the pan with the goose in it. "It's okay, boys, let it burn. The goose is done, so let's eat."

The men dropped their shovels and retrieved their mess kits. The commotion hadn't gone unnoticed, and before long, they were sharing that goose with all the men from the other guns of the battery, along with a few bottles of wine Davidson had stashed away in his duffel bag. It was the best meal they could recall going back to Brussels.

They would travel over three hundred miles through periods of rain, snow, sunshine, and wind, arriving at Nahrendorf on April 29 where they were assigned to the Ninth Army. There, they set up and fired on targets across the Elbe River. At 1255 hours on May 1, the last round was fired by Battery C, Gun Four. The battalion had fired over fifteen thousand rounds during their time in the field starting with the first shell launched by Battery A, Gun One at Heistern.

With the Russians coming from the north, many of the German civilians were trying to cross the Elbe River to escape being under their control. They were not allowed to cross and had to be turned back and relocated. Liberated Allied POWs and forced labor from every country caused a congestion the battalion never had to deal with before. The main task was segregating these forced laborers from the POWs and finding work for the captured Germans to do. In most cases, the POWs were assigned to KP duty, which to the surprise of everyone, they were actually quite good at.

A school was converted into a makeshift hospital so the Allied doctors could treat the many wounded German POWs as well as address the elderly civilian population who were suffering from malnutrition, scurvy, and pneumonia. Many of the children had lice, and diarrhea was a major concern because of the contaminated drinking water in Garlitz.

For the men of the 678th, the war was virtually over as their attention was now on running a town, caring for the POWs, and providing humanitarian aid to the hundreds of civilian refugees who were trapped in the village. Jim and the members of Gun One were assigned to run the kitchen and feed the members of their battalion using the POWs who were on permanent KP duty. The battalion mess crew joined other divisional messes who had turned their attention to feeding the civilians and those in the hospital.

"Hey, Jim, do you suppose we got this job because of the goose incident?" asked Otto.

"Yes, I would imagine that little trick was fresh on their mind," answered Jim. "But the major said that as long as we don't eat better than the officers, we can fix whatever we want and this assignment has got to be better than the other guys who are cleaning up the mess out there."

It was on May 9, 1945, that the official announcement of V-E Day or Victory in Europe was announced. The war was over. There was no formal celebration planned. The men were issued their new Eisenhower jackets and ordered to quickly change into them and meet on the main road. Each man cleaned up as best they could, changed into his dress A uniform, and with his pocket prayer book in hand assembled on the road. From there, the entire battalion marched as one to attend church services. They attended church as a unit to give thanks, pray for those who were not going home and of course, for the men who were still struggling in the Pacific against the Japanese.

As the men entered the building, they looked up to see, standing in the doorway, Captain Dallas, who had recovered from his wounds and who had been reassigned back with the battalion.

"This is a very good day," said Lad as he reached out and took the captain's hand.

Jim smiled as he saluted the captain and then removed his cover. "Welcome back, sir, we are glad to have you with us once again."

The captain greeted each man from Battery C. The sunglasses he was wearing weren't just to shield his eyes from the sun but to conceal the tears of joy and the pride he had for the men he once commanded and all they had accomplished.

"Yes, this is indeed a very good day," said the captain as he followed the last man into the makeshift chapel.

Chapter 18

GOING HOME

With the war over, the men's thoughts turned to home and just how soon they would be heading that way. The problem was everyone who enlisted or had been drafted was in until the end of hostilities, plus one year. There were hundreds of thousands of troops now in occupied Europe and a plan needed to be devised to start sending some home. The war in the Pacific was still going on, and even though the belief was it would end soon, the military had to make sure they had the troop strength to support that effort as well as maintain the peace in Europe. So with that in mind, they introduced the point system for determining who and when one would be separated.

Each man would be different. Points were awarded for how many times they were wounded. Certain medals were awarded for how long one had been in combat, but most of the points would be based on how long one had been in the service. The magic number a soldier needed to get his ticket punched to go home was eighty-five. If you had less than that number, then you stayed in Europe or you were preparing to ship to the Pacific Theater.

Jim and Lad were reviewing the point system to see just how much longer they had.

"Let's see," Jim said as he studied the guide. "Five points for campaign stars, twelve points for children up to three, five points for medals earned, one point for each month of our enlistment, and one point for every month we have been overseas."

Jim concluded he had earned, with his purple heart, sixty-seven points, and Lad was sixty-two.

"Eighteen more months," Jim said, a little dejected. "What in the hell will the army need me for that length of time?"

Lad figured he had two more years and said, "Well, I guess there isn't much we can do about it now. At least we don't have to spend more time sleeping with our guns."

Otto, who had joined them, said, "Maybe we should have gone along with their version of how we captured those Germans and taken the bronze star they wanted to give us. That would have added five points, and I would be down to a year."

Lad thought about what Otto said and concluded, "No, Digger, we couldn't do that. The boys that won those deserved them, and we didn't."

Otto responded, "I know, but it would be nice to get home before Christmas. It has been a long time since any of us has seen our families."

The battalion would not stay long in this location as they would be relieved by a quartermaster battalion who would take over the area. For the first time since they came ashore in France, the 678th would be separated. Headquarters and service battery would move to Lubtheen, A Battery to Quassel, B to Gudrow, and C would occupy Garlitz. It was at Garlitz that Plunger, Hollywood, and Yankee discovered a German prince and his family still living in their estate who, up until the war's end, had been under guard by the Germans. It wasn't long before MPs arrived, secured, and relieved the battery of any further duties relating to the prince.

* * * *

Back home, most of the sacrifices that had been made to accommodate the war effort were relaxing, and items that had once been rationed were now available without restrictions. John Deere was turning its attention to the manufacturing of farm equipment and was eager to hire the returning veterans to fulfill the orders that would be coming in.

The news coming from the Pacific was difficult because of the extreme measures the Japanese had taken to continue their effort to wage war. Ships were being attacked and sunk by suicide bombers known as kamikazes. These suicide missions were flown by young college students recruited and trained to fly one mission resulting in their death and the destruction of the U.S. ships they flew into.

Art was serving on board the destroyer Halligan. His ship was a part of a massive fleet steaming for the invasion of Okinawa, the gateway to the heart of the Japanese Empire. They were part of the fire support unit that arrived off the southern part of Okinawa on March 25 and began their patrol between Okinawa and Kerama. In addition to her other duties, the ship conducted minesweeper operations through waters which had been heavily mined with irregular patterns of explosives.

Art, along with the officers and men of his ship, was conducting a routine sweep when at 1835 hours, a tremendous explosion rocked the ship, sending smoke and debris two hundred feet in the air. The destroyer had hit a moored mine head on, exploding the forward magazines and blowing off the forward section of the ship, including the bridge back to the forward stack. Those who had not been killed or blown into the water were given the order to abandon ship by the lone surviving senior officer. Men threw themselves into the warm waters as the smoking ship drifted helplessly in the water.

The abandoned destroyer drifted aground on Tokashiki, a small island west of Okinawa, the following day. The destroyer Halligan, veteran of so many important operations in the Pacific, lost half of her crew of three hundred in the disaster, and only two of her twenty-one officers survived.

Art wrote in a letter later to his mother that he and a few of his shipmates were rescued by three marines who had seen the explosion and raced to their rescue in a makeshift boat they had discovered on the island. His letter went on to say that the young marine who reached him, by the name of Robert "Bob" Long, was also from Iowa. He forgot the town he was from but thought it ironic to be so far from home and yet so close because of the man who saved him.

Art was lucky compared with so many of his shipmates because, with the exception of having most of his clothing burnt or blown off, he had escaped with minor injuries and some second-degree burns. For Art, the war had come to an end, and he was expected, much to the relief of his mother and Anna, to be home in a few short months.

The determination of the Japanese military to carry on this fight regardless of the cost was causing great concern to President Truman. On Iwo Jima, the fight to gain control of that piece of land cost the marines 26,000 casualties, including 6,800 deaths. With the extreme measures the Japanese were employing, President Truman made the decision that would not only change the course of the war but would change the way the war could be waged in the future.

News swept quickly through every community as citizens gathered around their radio to listen to the president's announcement.

Hazel, Anna, and Mary listened closely to the president as he spoke. "Sixteen hours ago, an American airplane dropped one bomb on

Hiroshima and destroyed its usefulness to the enemy. That bomb had more power than twenty thousand tons of TNT. It had more than two thousand times the blast power of the British "Grand Slam" which is the largest bomb ever yet used in the history of warfare. The Japanese began the war from the air at Pearl Harbor. They have been repaid many fold. And the end is not yet. With this bomb, we have now added a new and revolutionary increase in destruction to supplement the growing power of our armed forces. In their present form, these bombs are now in production, and even more powerful forms are in development.

"It is an atomic bomb. It is a harnessing of the basic power of the universe. The force from which the sun draws its power has been lost against those who brought war to the Far East. If they do not now accept our terms, they may expect a rain of ruin from the air, the likes of which has never been seen on this earth. Behind this air attack will follow sea and land forces in such numbers and power that they have not yet seen and with the fighting skill of which they are already well aware."

The Japanese failed to meet the terms or the deadline for their unconditional surrender. So on August 9, the order went forward for the pilot and crew of the Enola Gay to once again drop its only other operational atomic bomb on Nagasaki. Forty thousand people died as a result, and on August 14, the Empire of Japan surrendered unconditionally. V-J day, the official end of World War II had finally arrived much to the joy and relief of a nation and a world who had endured so much.

* * * *

Anna listened to the news and could not believe what she had just heard. Outside, church bells were ringing, car horns were blaring, and sounds of people could be heard.

"Is it true it's finally over?" Anna asked Mary.

With tears in their eyes, they hugged each other, not wanting to let go but also wanting to go outside and listen and watch the spontaneous celebration that was going on in their neighborhood.

Anna knew that her dad, because of his age and his combined service in both wars, would soon be home. Now with the war being over, she wondered how much longer Jim would be needed before he could come home.

Hazel knew that her husband would also be home soon. He was recovering in a hospital in California from wounds he suffered during the battle at Iwo Jima. Daryl was on the side of Mount Suribachi along with his rifle platoon trying to get to the top. They were taking fire, and they were pinned down, not able to move up and not able to go down. He was hit in the leg, and a young sergeant named Bob Keeshan, a man who would later go on television as Captain Kangaroo and entertain children from 1955 to 1984, came to his aid. He directed the field of fire on the enemy position allowing the medics to get Daryl off the mountain.

That evening, Anna sat on her front porch and looked out over the neighborhood. Like not so long ago, there were children running through the fallen leaves, laughing and playing, while their moms were inside preparing supper. She looked over to the empty chair that Jim always sat in and started to cry. It was over, and just as Jim said, they soon would have the opportunity to have their lives together and raise their children.

* * * *

Jim, along with most of the men from his Battery, was back in Reims, France. They did not know at this point if they were going to be shipped to the Pacific. There was a rumor that they, being a bastard unit, would go stateside for additional training and then ship to the Pacific for the invasion of Japan. Jim knew if they had to stay, they were hoping they would keep their current assignment as a part of the occupational force of Europe.

The last thing they thought was that the men of the 678th would be assigned to other units, and their battalion would be busted up. That is, of course, what happened.

Battery C traded their weapons in for pots, pans, and serving utensils. Jim was promoted to staff sergeant and was placed in charge of a quartermaster section. His new assignment put him in charge of the food service for the troops in the village. It was an easy assignment, as the cooks came from the captured Germans who preferred peeling potatoes and boiling water to sitting in an old hut behind barbed wire and armed guards.

Jim became friends with a German named Kurt Arieser, who in civilian life was an art teacher at a local university outside of Berlin. He was married with three boys, and he had not seen his family for seven years. He stood over six feet and three inches and probably weighed well over two hundred and twenty pounds. He was very soft-spoken, and his English was broken but understandable. The two spoke of home, family, the future, and Jim understood they both just wanted to go back to the lives they had before this all started.

Kurt wondered if his village was spared from the bombardment of the Allied planes, if he even had a home or family to return to. He knew he would drive himself crazy if he didn't get his mind on something else. So when he was not in the kitchen preparing a meal with the other German prisoners, he was drawing scenery and portraits of the men wearing their Eisenhower jackets or anything else to keep his mind on something other than his home and family.

The men would try to pay him something for his drawings, but he always would smile and say, "One day, can you reduce my stay here by one day so I can go home? I think not, so today, it will be my pleasure but no refunds if you don't like them." And then he would laugh as he picked up his pencil and paper and went back to his work.

So much of Germany, as well as Russia and many other places in Europe, were destroyed, and it was going to take a massive effort on the part of the victorious countries to return the life for so many back to some sort of normal. Germany was divided in two, with the Eastern part being occupied and controlled by the Russians and the Western under the control of the U.S., British, and the French. The capital city of Berlin was also divided the same way, with East Berlin going to the Soviets.

The immediate goal was to reestablish basic needs to sustain life. Electricity, running water, roads, housing, and the effort to clean up the massive destruction left from the ordinance that demolished these once thriving communities. The marshall plan, named after General George C. Marshall who designed the plan immediately following the war, was part of the U.S. policy of containment with the focus of keeping communism from spreading. It was the U.S. hopes to quickly help the countries of Europe get back on their feet, stabilize their economy, and establish viable governments, so the citizens would not be tempted to adopt the system of communism.

* * * *

Most of the men knew that they didn't meet the point requirement for discharge, so with the weather turning cold, they prepared themselves for another winter. There was no talk of being home for Christmas, but maybe this year, they could actually decorate a tree and enjoy the holiday.

In the prisoners' compound, you could see and smell the smoke coming from the individual huts that provided them with some heat. Jim, who had not seen Kurt and he had not come to the kitchen the last couple of days, went along with Otto and Lad to the compound to see what was going on.

They found Kurt sitting on his cot reading a letter he had finally received from his wife. One look at his face, and you could see the news wasn't good. Jim asked if he wanted to talk, but instead of talking, he just handed him the letter. To Jim's surprise, it was written in English, so he read the words on the page. It was brief, but each word stung as he read the account of Kurt's son, all three of them. The youngest, just being fourteen, had been taken away by the SS and shipped to the Russian front. His wife Hannah had been writing to him for the last three years, and this was the first letter Kurt actually got. She went on to say that she was now alone and not doing well, and with winter coming she didn't know if she was going to make it if he didn't get home soon. Jim handed the letter back to Kurt, and he saw the helplessness and concern that was evident in his face and eyes.

"Come with me," Jim said as he reached for Kurt's arm. "This war is over for you."

Lad and Otto didn't say a word as they all walked back to the kitchen. They drank coffee and devised a plan that would get Kurt on his way home, hopefully within the next twenty-four to forty-eight hours. To get the plan put into action would take the cooperation of a lot of different men who are not only willing to help in the escape but were able to provide the things needed, and keep their mouths shut. They would need clothing to make Kurt look like a German citizen, papers allowing him passage through the different road blocks, transportation from Reims, France to his home outside Berlin, and food to sustain him for the five-hundred-seventy-six-mile trip home.

They all understood what they were doing would be subject to court-martial if caught. But their thoughts were not about what could happen to them but rather on the good they were doing for someone else. This man posed no threat to the security of the place; he wasn't a war criminal. He was just a soldier who had completed his duty, and now it was time for him to go home and get a new start.

Jim said, "Kurt, we are going to give you those days you asked us for when you drew our portraits."

Friday evening, they put their plan into motion. Jim, Lad, and Otto drove Kurt down to the train station. Lad went to the ticket counter and purchased a one-way ticket to Berlin. He showed the ticket agent papers they had drawn up allowing Kurt safe passage. Once he had the ticket, he walked back to the jeep where Otto, Jim, and Kurt were waiting. Goodbyes had to be said quickly, as they did not want to draw any suspension as to why three GIs were traveling with a German civilian.

Kurt shook each hand and said, "Thank you." He took Jim's hand and said, "My friend, how can I ever repay you for what you are doing for me?"

Jim squeezed his hand and said, "By going home and having a long and happy life with your wife and your family because I intend on doing the same."

Kurt replied, "I shall never forget any of you."

As he placed the ticket inside his coat, he pulled the knapsack filled with food out of the jeep, slung it over his shoulder, and walked to the train. He did not look back, as he didn't want to draw suspicion. Jim, Otto, and Lad waited to see him disappear onto the train and then drove their jeep back to their post.

Jim figured he would never know what happened to Kurt—if he made it or what happened to his family, but he was satisfied they got him home.

He would get a Christmas card sent to his home in December of 1949. It came addressed only as Sergeant James McManis, Ottumwa, Iowa. Inside was a photo of Kurt, his wife, and two of his sons. Apparently, one of his boys had died during the war. Kurt wanted Jim to know that he was not only grateful for his friendship and kindness but that he was fulfilling the promise he made when they departed not so many years ago and hoped Jim was doing the same.

* * * *

Jim was sitting in the dining room going over that day's menu when Captain Dallas entered for a cup of coffee.

Jim took a seat across from the captain when he said, "Sergeant McManis, we need to talk. I see a lot of good soldiering in you, and I would like you to consider making the army your life. It can be a good life, and now with the war over, it can provide a good stable life for a young man like you who is just starting his family. You're a good soldier, and the army is going to need soldiers like you. I want you to consider my proposal along with a promotion to first sergeant if you accept."

Jim was taken off guard by the proposal and did not respond right away. He looked at the captain as he thought about what was just said. He never really saw himself as a career soldier, and all he really wanted to do was to go home. It had been way too long since he held Anna, and he didn't ever want to be in a position where he would have to leave her again.

Finally, Jim spoke, "Sir, I really appreciate the offer and the confidence you have in my soldiering. But can you promise me that if I stay in the army, I won't have to leave my wife again?"

Captain Dallas had to say they both already knew that answer. So the captain stood up and said, "I need you, Sergeant Davison and Merringer, in the orderly room by 1300 hours today. It seems we are missing a German prisoner, and I am told you may have some helpful information as to his whereabouts."

Without saying another word or waiting for Jim's answer, he turned and walked out the door.

The three men sat in the orderly room waiting for the captain to call them in. They were not sure if they would go in one at a time, as a group, or what was going on. On their walk over, they had decided to be truthful and not try to make up a story and then try to remember it. They would answer the questions truthfully but not volunteer anything.

Finally, the technical sergeant told them they could go in. Jim went in first and stood at attention in front of Captain Dallas's desk. He was shuffling through some paper when he looked up and told them to stand at ease.

"Men, it has been reported that one of the prisoners from the lower compound went missing and that he was a cook for your mess. Would any of you know anything about this?"

Jim was the first to speak. "Sir, he shared a letter with me that he got from his wife. It apparently was the first letter he had received in seven years, and it concerned the welfare of his wife and the upcoming winter. I think he went home!"

The captain stood up and walked around his desk. He stopped in front of the other two men and said, "So, Sergeants, do you know anything more than that?"

"No, sir," was their quick response.

"So he just got a letter and walked off the post and went home?" "Yes, sir, that is how we see it," spoke Otto.

"Very well then. You and Sergeant Davidson are dismissed. McManis, I have a few more questions I need to ask of you, so I need you to stay so I can complete my official report."

Davidson and Merringer saluted and exited the office, allowing the door to close behind them.

"Have a seat, Sergeant," said Captain Dallas.

"It was reported that the prisoner might have gotten a little help with papers, clothing, and tickets, and your name has been associated with that help. Is there any truth to those rumors?"

Jim knew he was had, so he told the captain the entire story. Once he laid out the details and the reasoning behind their assistance, he said, "Sir, if there is to be any repercussions for this, they should include just me because Davidson and Merringer knew nothing."

The captain looked down at his report and said, "I don't see that any real harm has been done. It looks to me, we just lost track of one of the prisoners."

He went on to say, "With the war being over and based on his records, I don't think we can really consider him a prisoner. I see him as a person of interest, and if they need to find him or speak to him they can, since they have cataloged the homes of each detainee."

He paused as he looked over the report and said, "I don't see any reason why this event should alter or impact the otherwise exemplary record of a good soldier. The reports I have been given are sketchy to say the least, so as far as I am concerned, there is nothing the army needs to do at this time."

Jim sat quietly, not wanting to say anything more on the matter.

Finally, Captain Dallas broke the silence by saying, "Sergeant, I have sixty days to finalize my report and turn it into the battalion commander. As far as I am concerned, this case is closed. I appreciate your honesty, but I must insist, after you leave this room, there will be no further mention of this incident. They in headquarters may or may not agree with my assessment, but since I have the ability to start moving men stateside, I figure it a moot point if you, Davidson, and Merringer were no longer in Europe."

Jim couldn't believe what he just heard. Was he going home?

The captain continued, "Sergeant, I have made arrangements for you, as well as Davidson and Merringer, to leave tomorrow morning. The three of you will be leaving by train to England. You will be there about three to four days before you board a troop transport taking you to New York. Once there, you will be transported to Fort McCoy, Wisconsin. I would expect your stay to be brief, and once you have completed your exit physical, you will receive a debriefing prior to being discharged.

You have the gratitude of myself, this division, and a grateful nation for your service during this time of conflict. I suspect once discharged, you will be provided transportation and any pay owed to you for your trip back to Iowa and your family. None of you involved in these orders are to share this information with anyone, including your family, until you have reached the States. Do you understand these instructions?"

"Yes, sir," snapped Jim, trying to hide the biggest smile he had ever had but not doing a very good job of it.

Both men stood up as Captain Dallas reached for Jim's hand.

The captain who was also smiling now, said, "Arky, it was an honor to be your commander. I wish you well in whatever you decide to do from this day forward. I would imagine the army made you a better man, and I know you have made me a better commander."

Jim thanked the captain for all he had done, realizing this was really goodbye, and their paths may never cross again. But all he could think of was "oh my god, I am going home."

* * * *

Crossing the Atlantic in the late fall can be rough, and this crossing would be no exception. There were great swells that rocked and bounced the ship around like a toy boat in a bathtub. The vessel taking them home was not a military vessel but an American civilian cargo ship contracted by the military to transport men and equipment back to the States. The three men had no special routing or duties to perform, so they spent their time playing cards, drinking coffee, and sleeping. Occasionally, they would go up on deck to smoke their pipes when the smoking lamp was lit and watch the horizon or any site of land. Their thoughts were of where they had been and finally on home. They now could afford to allow their minds to think of home, a danger soldiers needed to avoid during war because any distraction could result in getting you killed. The air up on the deck was cold as it blew across, often accompanied by a spray of the water coming over the side. It was no place to linger long but necessary to break the boredom of a trip that seemed to be taking way too long.

It was 1700 hours on Wednesday, November 28, 1945, and everyone was on deck as the ship entered the harbor of New York City. In the distance, the men could see the Statue of Liberty. Her arm stretched to the sky, and unlike the first time they saw her, her torch glowed as if it was lit to welcome them home. It was a beautiful sight to see because it was not only a symbol of freedom, but it meant they were back in the good old United States.

"Give me your tired, your poor, your huddled masses yearning to breathe free," Lad said as they approached.

"Is it a call for those who wish to come here or is it a reminder for those returning of how lucky we are?" Jim asked.

Lad answered Jim's question by saying, "Who can look at her and not think of all the grandfathers and grandmothers who followed that light? They came from so many places because of the freedom she offered and the promise she would keep. She stands as a beacon of light for those who long to be free and burns even brighter for us who call her home."

Once in New York, the men's first stop was to a telegraph office to send messages home announcing their arrival. Jim grabbed a pencil from the cup on the counter and wrote the following message to Anna: "I am in New York City, stop. Won't be here long, stop. Do not try to contact me, stop. Will contact you soon, stop. Heading to Fort McCoy, Wisconsin, stop. I LOVE YOU!"

As the man looked over the message, he held his hand and said, "That will be one dollar."

"When will she get the message?" Jim asked as he pulled his wallet from his coat pocket.

"Tomorrow" was the response.

"Tomorrow," Jim repeated. He could imagine the excitement of the news and how Anna would start fussing over every little detail. She would start the preparation for his arrival, and he knew that she would be a little perturbed with his note because she did not know how much time she had.

Once they arrived at Fort McCoy, they started the process of becoming a civilian again. Each day seemed to be a week, and each week seemed as if it had extra days. Jim began the process by completing his physical, attending briefings, and of course, enduring the boredom as he waited for that final order to send him home. Each day, the men went to the orderly room and glanced at the names looking for discharge orders; and each day, they walked away hoping for better news tomorrow.

Finally on December 10, 1945, Jim saw his posting. His orders were in, and he would depart from La Crosse, Wisconsin, on Friday December 14 early evening and would be home by Saturday, sometime in the afternoon. He looked over to Lad and Otto only to discover they would have to wait another day as their names were not yet listed.

Jim broke the silence when he said, "How do I say goodbye? We have shared so much with each other, and I would imagine you two probably know me better than any other person in my life up to this point? You have stood by my side regardless of the circumstance, the danger, and your unwavering friendship was never in question nor will it ever be forgotten."

Lad smiled and said, "It's okay, Arky, you're getting a jump on us, but we will catch up with you soon enough. For now, let's head over to the club and you can buy the first round."

Otto laughed and said, "First round, my ass, he can buy all the rounds."

* * * *

Snow was falling as Jim boarded the train. He heard the conductor announce "All aboard" as the train whistle blew and the wheels started the slow process of moving this metal giant away from the station. It would be a short trip over to Chicago where he would change trains and take the Midwestern Zephyr into Ottumwa. As Jim looked out the window, enjoying the beauty of the Midwest, he noticed that the snow had picked up. He was hopeful that this snow would not delay his trip because a train never understood the idea of being on time, and it certainly didn't need any help from Mother Nature.

The snow had stopped, and the sun was peeking through overcast skies as the train came around a small curve, running along the Des Moines River. Jim glanced out the window to see the sign "Ottumwa." He was almost home. It had been over three years since he had been home, and the excitement was starting to build knowing it was finally over. The train slowed down to a crawl as it pulled into the station, and Jim saw through his window Anna, Craig, Art, Mary, and his dad who was holding a small Irish flag in one hand and an American flag in the other, standing on the platform.

There was no way for Jim to know, but at home under the Christmas tree was one special package for him. It was the scrapbook Anna had given him on their first Christmas back in 1941. It now was filled with photos, orders, newspaper accounts, and memories of the journey they had taken together during the war. The very last entry was of course the telegram announcing that he was back in the States.

Jim gathered his things as he looked at the people waiting for him and thought of where he had been, what he had experienced, and how it had changed him. He was straightening his uniform when he realized he had not mentioned the Purple Heart he was displaying along with the other medals he was awarded during the war. He knew he would be in trouble for not mentioning them but hoped that their seeing him standing before them would be proof enough that he was just fine. For now, all that mattered was that he was home, and he couldn't wait to get off the train and sweep Anna into his arms.

He also couldn't wait to share the two bottles of champagne that Captain Dallas had put in his duffel bag. Who knows, maybe even Mary, who never drank, might just indulge in the moment and share a glass.

Jim knew it was over; he was home, and the life he and Anna had put on hold was no longer a hope but was a reality of the vision they shared from the day they said, "I do."